Eating on the Spectrum

From ARFID to PICA

Gareth Croot

Contents

Chapter 1

Introduction to Eating Disorders on the Autism Spectrum

Eating behaviors are essential to overall health, yet for individuals on the autism spectrum, food-related challenges can present profound complexities. Unlike typical eating disorders like anorexia or bulimia, the eating difficulties experienced by those on the autism spectrum often stem from unique sensory, behavioral, and cognitive patterns, making their manifestations distinct and, at times, difficult to understand. This chapter will provide an overview of these eating challenges, setting the foundation for understanding conditions such as Avoidant/Restrictive Food Intake Disorder (ARFID) and PICA, which are more common in those with Autism Spectrum Disorder (ASD) than in the general population.

1.1 The Prevalence of Eating Disorders in ASD

Eating challenges are prevalent among individuals on the autism spectrum. Studies show that up to 70% of autistic children experience feeding or eating difficulties, a significantly higher rate than in neurotypical children. While most children experience picky eating at some point, many on the spectrum develop a deep-rooted attachment or aversion to specific foods that can last well into adulthood. For some, these issues intensify into conditions like ARFID or PICA, which are not merely picky eating behaviors but are classified as severe eating disorders requiring specialized attention.

1.2 The Role of Sensory Processing Differences

A defining factor of eating disorders in ASD is the role of sensory processing differences. Individuals on the spectrum frequently experience heightened or diminished sensitivities to sensory inputs—such as taste, texture, smell, and appearance—which can profoundly affect their food choices. For instance, someone with heightened sensory sensitivity may find the texture of certain foods unbearable, causing them to avoid entire food groups. In contrast, an individual with a reduced sensitivity may prefer intense flavors or crunchy textures to stimulate their senses. This sensitivity to texture, taste, smell, and even color often results in a very restricted diet.

1.3 Behavioral Patterns and Rigid Preferences

Another layer of complexity in ASD-related eating disorders is the role of behavioral rigidity and preferences. Many individuals on the spectrum exhibit repetitive behaviors and routines, which can extend to their eating habits. They may insist on eating the same foods every day or only eat foods prepared in a specific way. Changes in mealtime routines or the appearance of a meal can cause extreme distress, leading to avoidance of food altogether. This need for consistency can make dietary expansion challenging and may limit nutritional intake.

1.4 Distinction from Traditional Eating Disorders

Traditional eating disorders like anorexia and bulimia are often driven by body image concerns or a desire for control over one's body. In contrast, eating disorders in ASD are generally not linked to body image issues. Instead, they arise from sensory sensitivities, anxiety, and a need for routine and predictability. For example, while someone with anorexia might restrict food to lose weight, an individual with ARFID may restrict food due to a strong aversion to the sensory characteristics of certain foods. Recognizing this difference is crucial to understanding the unique approaches needed to support individuals on the spectrum.

1.5 Common Eating Disorders Associated with ASD

Among the eating disorders prevalent in ASD, ARFID and PICA stand out as particularly challenging:

- **Avoidant/Restrictive Food Intake Disorder (ARFID):** Characterized by a limited intake of food due to sensory aversions, lack of interest in eating, or fear of adverse effects (such as choking). Individuals with ARFID may have an extremely restricted diet, which can lead to nutritional deficiencies.

- **PICA:** Defined by the persistent eating of non-food substances, such as dirt, paper, or hair. PICA is often seen in autistic individuals and can pose severe health risks, such as gastrointestinal issues and poisoning, depending on the ingested substance.
-

While these are among the most commonly diagnosed eating disorders on the spectrum, many individuals also experience less well-defined but equally impactful eating challenges, often characterized by severe food selectivity or extreme avoidance of certain food types.

1.6 Why Early Intervention Matters

The impact of these eating disorders can extend beyond the immediate physical consequences of nutritional deficiencies or gastrointestinal issues. Malnutrition can impair cognitive and physical development, especially in children, while the social isolation caused by restricted diets can affect psychological well-being. Early intervention is essential for minimizing these risks, as it can help develop positive eating habits, increase food tolerance, and address underlying sensory or behavioral issues.

1.7 The Importance of a Multidisciplinary Approach

Addressing eating disorders on the autism spectrum often requires a multidisciplinary approach involving pediatricians, psychologists, occupational therapists, and nutritionists. Each professional brings a different perspective, with occupational therapists focusing on sensory integration, psychologists addressing behavioral concerns, and nutritionists guiding balanced diets. Family involvement is also critical, as caregivers are often the first to notice patterns and can support positive mealtime habits.

1.8 Moving Forward

In the chapters that follow, we will explore the unique facets of ARFID, PICA, and other eating challenges on the autism spectrum. We will examine diagnostic criteria, therapeutic interventions, and coping strategies, equipping readers with a comprehensive understanding of how to support individuals with these complex needs. Understanding these challenges as a spectrum themselves—varying widely from person to person—will be key as we journey through the intricacies of eating on the spectrum.

Chapter 2

What is ARFID?

Avoidant/Restrictive Food Intake Disorder (ARFID) is an eating disorder characterized by a highly selective intake of food, often driven by sensory sensitivities, fear of negative consequences like choking or vomiting, or an overall lack of interest in eating. Unlike other eating disorders, ARFID is not associated with concerns about body weight or shape. Instead, it is often influenced by unique factors, particularly in individuals on the autism spectrum. In this chapter, we will explore the symptoms, diagnostic criteria, and the significant impact ARFID has on those with Autism Spectrum Disorder (ASD).

2.1 Defining ARFID in the Context of Autism

ARFID is a relatively new addition to the Diagnostic and Statistical Manual of Mental Disorders (DSM-5), where it is defined by restrictive eating that causes nutritional deficits, weight loss, or dependence on supplements. For individuals with autism, ARFID can be particularly challenging, as their experiences of food are often shaped by sensory sensitivities, heightened anxiety, and a need for routine, making food intake restrictive and inflexible.

For individuals with ASD, ARFID often manifests through an extremely limited diet that may lack variety and essential nutrients. Rather than being driven by body image issues, as seen in anorexia or bulimia, the restriction in ARFID often results from sensory aversions to certain tastes, textures, colors, or smells, as well as fears of potential adverse reactions, such as choking or gastrointestinal distress. These unique drivers make ARFID in ASD an especially complex condition to address.

2.2 Symptoms of ARFID

ARFID symptoms can vary, but there are common signs that clinicians and caregivers can observe.
These include:
- **Extremely selective eating**: Individuals may refuse entire categories of food, limiting their diet to just a few "safe" foods, such as plain carbohydrates or specific brands and types of packaged foods.

- **Fear of adverse consequences**: Some individuals with ARFID develop a fear of eating due to concerns about choking, gagging, or vomiting. This fear can lead to significant anxiety around food and may limit food intake to only very soft or bland items.
- **Reliance on supplements or tube feeding**: Due to nutritional gaps caused by limited food intake, some individuals may require supplements or, in severe cases, tube feeding to maintain adequate nutrition.
- **Low body weight and poor growth**: Restricted food intake often leads to weight loss, malnutrition, or stunted growth, particularly in children and adolescents who need a wide variety of nutrients for healthy development.
- **Anxiety or distress around mealtime**: Individuals with ARFID may exhibit stress, frustration, or resistance around mealtimes, especially if they are expected to try new or disliked foods.

These symptoms significantly impact quality of life, not only because of the health implications of nutritional deficiencies but also due to the social and emotional toll of restricted eating.

2.3 The Impact of Sensory Sensitivities on ARFID in ASD

Sensory processing differences are a hallmark of ASD, and for many, sensory sensitivities play a central role in ARFID. Autistic individuals may be hypersensitive or hyposensitive to various sensory stimuli, including the taste, smell, texture, and appearance of foods. For someone with hypersensitivity, certain textures (e.g., slimy or crunchy) or flavors (e.g., sour or bitter) can be overwhelming or even unbearable, leading them to avoid foods that trigger these responses.

Moreover, these sensitivities often create a strong reliance on specific "safe" foods, which have predictable sensory characteristics. This can lead to a cycle where the individual is resistant to trying new foods because they lack the predictability and comfort that safe foods provide. For caregivers, understanding these sensory sensitivities is crucial to supporting individuals with ARFID, as pushing new foods too quickly can increase anxiety and further entrench restrictive eating behaviors.

2.4 Psychological Factors Contributing to ARFID

In addition to sensory sensitivities, psychological factors like anxiety and the need for routine significantly contribute to ARFID in individuals with ASD. Fear of negative consequences, such as choking or vomiting, can lead to food avoidance and may cause individuals to avoid even familiar foods if they are prepared in a different way. This can create high levels of stress around mealtime, which may only further reinforce restrictive eating habits.

The strong preference for routine that is common in ASD can also make it difficult for individuals to accept dietary changes. They may refuse to eat if they're presented with a new food, if a food looks different than usual, or if it's offered in a different setting. These rigid preferences can make ARFID management particularly challenging, as attempts to diversify the diet may be met with strong resistance.

2.5 The Physical and Social Impact of ARFID

The physical health consequences of ARFID in ASD can be profound. Malnutrition, vitamin deficiencies, and low energy levels are common among individuals with severely restricted diets. In children and adolescents, these nutritional deficits can hinder physical growth, cognitive development, and immune function. Poor nutritional intake can also exacerbate symptoms of ASD, such as irritability and difficulty concentrating, creating a cycle where poor nutrition negatively impacts overall well-being. In addition to physical health consequences, ARFID can lead to social isolation. Individuals with ARFID often avoid social settings that involve food, such as family meals, birthday parties, and gatherings. This isolation can affect social relationships and limit opportunities for social development, which can already be a challenge for those with ASD. As they mature, individuals with ARFID may face additional barriers in forming relationships, attending school, or engaging in community activities.

2.6 Diagnosis of ARFID

Diagnosing ARFID in individuals with ASD requires a careful assessment by a healthcare professional who can differentiate ARFID from typical eating difficulties seen in autism. A comprehensive evaluation may involve physical exams, nutritional assessments, and questionnaires designed to understand eating behaviors and their underlying causes. The diagnosis often requires input from multiple professionals, including psychologists, dietitians, and occupational therapists, to address the complex sensory, psychological, and nutritional aspects of the disorder.

2.7 Treatment Approaches for ARFID

Managing ARFID in ASD requires a multidisciplinary approach that takes into account the individual's unique sensory and psychological needs.
Treatment often involves:

- **Behavioral therapy**: Techniques such as cognitive-behavioral therapy (CBT) and exposure therapy can help individuals gradually accept a wider variety of foods and manage anxiety around eating.
- **Sensory integration therapy**: Occupational therapists may work with individuals to reduce sensory sensitivities through sensory integration techniques, which can help them feel more comfortable with different textures and tastes.
- **Nutritional counseling**: Dietitians can help identify and address nutrient deficiencies and create a gradual plan to expand the individual's diet.
- **Parental support and training**: Family involvement is crucial in ARFID management, as parents and caregivers play an essential role in creating a positive, low-stress mealtime environment and providing gentle encouragement to try new foods.

2.8 Moving Forward with a Better Understanding of ARFID

Understanding ARFID in the context of autism is essential for creating supportive and effective strategies for those affected. By recognizing the unique sensory, psychological, and behavioral factors that contribute to this eating disorder, caregivers and healthcare professionals can foster a more compassionate and individualized approach to treatment. In the following chapters, we will explore other eating disorders, such as PICA, as well as additional strategies and tools for managing eating challenges on the spectrum. Through patience, tailored support, and understanding, individuals with ARFID can achieve progress toward healthier and more varied eating habits.

Chapter 3

What is PICA?

PICA is an eating disorder characterized by the compulsive urge to consume non-food items, such as dirt, paper, chalk, or hair, which can pose significant health risks. While it can affect individuals of all ages and neurotypes, PICA is particularly prevalent among those with developmental conditions, including Autism Spectrum Disorder (ASD). In this chapter, we will explore the symptoms, potential triggers, and implications of PICA in people with ASD, as well as approaches for managing this challenging condition.

3.1 Defining PICA in the Context of Autism

PICA is defined by the persistent eating of substances that are not considered food and have no nutritional value. To meet the diagnostic criteria, the behavior must persist for at least one month and be developmentally inappropriate (meaning it is not typical for very young children who are naturally inclined to explore objects by mouthing them). Among individuals with ASD, PICA is often observed due to a variety of sensory, psychological, and behavioral factors, and it can range from occasional ingestion to a consistent, ingrained behavior.
For individuals with autism, PICA often extends beyond typical behaviors associated with curiosity or exploration. It can become a habitual or even compulsive act, driven by sensory needs, environmental influences, or a lack of impulse control. PICA can pose serious health risks, such as poisoning, gastrointestinal blockages, infections, and dental damage, especially when the ingested substances are hazardous.

3.2 Symptoms of PICA

PICA presents through the consumption of non-food items, and the substances ingested can vary widely. Some common items include:
- **Earth-based materials**: Dirt, clay, sand, and chalk.
- **Paper products**: Tissue paper, cardboard, and books.
- **Household items**: Soap, hair, fabric, and plastic.
- **Metal and stones**: Nails, pebbles, coins, or other small, hard objects.

People with PICA often exhibit a preference for specific non-food items, which may be tied to particular sensory experiences. For example, a person might favor crunchy items like gravel, or soft, pliable items like clay. These behaviors can become so ingrained that the individual actively seeks out the items to fulfill a sensory craving or to reduce stress.

3.3 Triggers and Contributing Factors of PICA in ASD

For individuals on the autism spectrum, the behaviors associated with PICA may arise from multiple interrelated factors, including sensory processing differences, behavioral patterns, and psychological needs:

- **Sensory Processing Needs**: Sensory processing difficulties are a core feature of autism and can significantly influence eating behaviors. In the case of PICA, some individuals may find specific textures, temperatures, or smells of non-food items appealing. This sensory-seeking behavior can make certain non-food items particularly attractive, especially if they provide a sense of comfort or stimulation that the individual craves.
- **Behavioral Patterns and Routines**: People with ASD often develop repetitive behaviors or routines that provide comfort or predictability. For some, consuming certain non-food items becomes a ritual that is difficult to disrupt. This pattern may intensify over time, as the individual increasingly relies on these behaviors to manage anxiety or sensory needs.
- **Anxiety and Self-Soothing**: For some individuals with ASD, PICA can serve as a coping mechanism for managing anxiety or emotional discomfort. The act of eating or mouthing non-food items may provide a calming effect or help redirect focus away from stressful stimuli. When PICA behaviors are reinforced as a way to manage distress, they can become more persistent and difficult to break.

- **Intellectual and Developmental Challenges**: Cognitive and developmental differences in some individuals with ASD may lead to difficulties in understanding the consequences of eating non-food items, such as health risks or social inappropriateness. This can make it harder for them to control or avoid PICA behaviors without guidance and intervention.

3.4 Health Implications of PICA

The health risks associated with PICA are significant and can vary based on the types of items ingested:
- **Gastrointestinal Issues**: Ingesting hard or sharp items can lead to gastrointestinal blockages, perforations, or tears, which may require surgical intervention.
- **Poisoning**: Some ingested items, such as paint chips or certain plants, may contain toxic substances that can lead to poisoning. This is particularly concerning with items like lead-based paint, which can cause neurological damage.
- **Infections**: Consuming dirt, feces, or other contaminated substances can introduce harmful bacteria or parasites into the body, resulting in infections that may require medical treatment.
- **Dental Damage**: Biting or chewing on hard objects, such as stones or metal, can cause dental fractures, wear down teeth, or lead to oral infections.

The health risks are substantial, and the consequences of PICA behaviors often require immediate and ongoing medical attention. Understanding these risks can help caregivers and professionals prioritize interventions to protect the health and safety of individuals with PICA.

3.5 Diagnosis of PICA

Diagnosing PICA in individuals with ASD requires a comprehensive assessment by a healthcare professional, often involving physical exams, nutritional evaluations, and psychological assessments. The diagnostic process aims to distinguish PICA from other sensory-seeking or exploratory behaviors and to understand the underlying factors contributing to the behavior.
Assessing the individual's sensory needs, psychological state, and environmental factors is essential in developing a tailored intervention plan. In some cases, additional tests such as X-rays or blood work may be necessary to detect any complications, like blockages or toxic substance exposure.

3.6 Treatment Approaches for PICA

Managing PICA requires a multidisciplinary approach that addresses the underlying causes, meets the individual's sensory needs, and provides strategies for redirecting behaviors:

- **Behavioral Therapy**: Behavioral interventions, such as Applied Behavior Analysis (ABA), are often used to help individuals replace PICA behaviors with safer, more appropriate alternatives. These approaches can include positive reinforcement for avoiding non-food items and gradual desensitization to reduce reliance on these behaviors.
- **Sensory Integration Therapy**: Sensory integration therapy, typically led by an occupational therapist, can help individuals meet their sensory needs in safer ways. This may involve offering alternative sensory experiences, such as chewing on safe, textured items or engaging in sensory play activities that provide similar stimulation to the items they crave.
- **Environmental Modifications**: Modifying the individual's environment to limit access to non-food items can help reduce the risk of PICA behaviors. This might include securing hazardous items, using visual cues to indicate items that are off-limits, or providing a structured environment that reduces opportunities for PICA.

- **Nutritional Interventions**: In cases where PICA may be related to nutritional deficiencies (such as iron deficiency), a registered dietitian can help create a balanced diet that reduces cravings. Supplements may be recommended under medical supervision if certain deficiencies are suspected to contribute to PICA.
- **Parental and Caregiver Training**: Training for parents and caregivers is critical in managing PICA, as they are essential in monitoring behaviors, reinforcing safe alternatives, and ensuring a supportive environment. Techniques to manage PICA-related behaviors, like redirection and positive reinforcement, can make a significant difference when implemented consistently at home.

3.7 Long-Term Considerations for Managing PICA

While treatment can reduce PICA behaviors, long-term management may still be necessary, as sensory needs and behavioral patterns often persist. Developing coping skills, providing ongoing sensory support, and monitoring for potential triggers can help individuals maintain progress and reduce the risk of relapse. Encouraging safe alternatives and involving the individual in choices can also pomote autonomy and better adherence to interventions.

3.8 Moving Forward

PICA is a complex and potentially hazardous behavior that requires a nuanced approach to address both the individual's sensory needs and their behavioral patterns. By understanding the triggers and contributing factors, caregivers and professionals can create a comprehensive support plan that promotes health and safety. As we continue through this book, we will explore further strategies, conditions, and interventions relevant to the eating challenges faced by those on the autism spectrum, equipping readers with the tools to better support and empower individuals with PICA and other related disorders.

Chapter 4: Beyond ARFID and PICA: Other Eating Challenges

While ARFID and PICA are well-known eating challenges for individuals with Autism Spectrum Disorder (ASD), many other eating behaviors and preferences arise from the unique sensory and psychological characteristics associated with autism. In this chapter, we'll delve into common eating challenges beyond ARFID and PICA, such as hypersensitivity to sensory inputs, rigidity around food, and the need for routines, all of which impact dietary habits, nutrition, and overall well-being.

4.1 Sensory Hypersensitivity and Food Aversion

One of the most common eating challenges for individuals with ASD is hypersensitivity to sensory stimuli related to food, which can create strong aversions to certain textures, smells, tastes, or even colors of foods. This sensory hypersensitivity leads to avoidance behaviors that can result in a highly restricted diet, impacting the individual's overall nutrition.

- **Texture Sensitivity**: Many individuals with ASD are particularly sensitive to textures, which can lead to preferences for certain types of foods (e.g., only crunchy or only soft foods) and a complete aversion to others. For example, an individual may refuse all fruits with a mushy texture or dislike any vegetables that have a fibrous consistency.
- **Smell and Taste Sensitivity**: Strong flavors or particular smells may be overwhelming, even in small amounts. The smell of certain cooked vegetables, spices, or dairy products can be so aversive that individuals may refuse to eat not only the offending food but anything that has been prepared in the same kitchen environment.
- **Visual Sensitivity**: Some individuals may even be sensitive to the color or appearance of food. For example, they might avoid foods with mixed colors or refuse to eat items that do not look "perfect." This level of sensitivity can be a barrier to trying new or nutritionally diverse foods.

This heightened sensory experience makes mealtime challenging for both individuals with ASD and their caregivers. Often, caregivers must balance the need to provide adequate nutrition with the individual's specific sensory requirements, finding creative ways to offer foods that align with these preferences.

4.2 Food Rigidity and the Need for Routine

Rigid eating habits are another common challenge among individuals with ASD. This rigidity often manifests as a need for consistency in types of food, food brands, preparation methods, and even specific mealtime routines.

- **Brand Specificity**: Many individuals with ASD prefer specific brands or types of foods due to their predictability in taste, texture, or appearance. If a favorite brand is unavailable or changes its formula, it can be distressing and lead to refusal of that food item.
- **Routines Around Mealtime**: Individuals with ASD often find comfort in routines, which can extend to how and when they eat. For instance, they may insist on eating in a particular order, at a specific time, or even using the same plate and utensils. Any deviation from this routine can cause stress or a refusal to eat.
- **Limited Repertoire of Foods**: Individuals may become fixated on a small selection of foods, often those that meet specific sensory needs, and refuse anything outside this "safe" list. This rigidity can lead to a lack of variety in the diet, potentially resulting in nutrient deficiencies.

The inflexibility around food choices and routines can significantly impact family dynamics, especially when caregivers try to introduce new foods or encourage healthier options. Addressing food rigidity requires patience and gradual, gentle exposure to new foods without disrupting the individual's sense of comfort and routine.

4.3 Oral-Motor Challenges and Difficulty with Chewing or Swallowing

Some individuals on the autism spectrum experience difficulties with oral-motor skills, which can affect their ability to chew and swallow properly. These challenges can make eating a physically uncomfortable or even distressing experience.

- **Chewing Difficulties**: Chewing requires fine motor control, which can be challenging for individuals with developmental delays or motor skill difficulties. They may avoid foods that are hard to chew, like meats, certain fruits, or crunchy vegetables, and prefer foods that require minimal effort to consume.
- **Swallowing Sensitivities**: Some individuals with ASD may have heightened awareness of the swallowing process, which can lead to a fear of choking or gagging. This can cause avoidance of foods that require multiple chews or foods that are thick or sticky, such as peanut butter or bananas.
- **Texture Modification for Safety and Comfort**: Due to these challenges, many caregivers modify food textures to make eating easier and more comfortable, such as pureeing fruits and vegetables or opting for softer foods. This approach helps maintain nutritional intake without causing physical discomfort or distress around eating.

4.4 Avoidance of Mixed or Unfamiliar Foods

Many individuals with ASD display an aversion to mixed or unfamiliar foods, a behavior that aligns with a broader need for predictability and control.

- **Dislike of Mixed Foods**: This aversion can be particularly strong when it comes to dishes with mixed textures or multiple ingredients, such as casseroles, soups, or salads. The unpredictability of combined flavors or textures can make these dishes overwhelming and unappealing.

- **Reluctance to Try New Foods**: New foods can provoke anxiety or suspicion, as the unfamiliarity disrupts the sense of control or predictability that many individuals with ASD rely on. This reluctance can extend to anything that doesn't match their mental "blueprint" of acceptable food, even if it's a slight variation of a familiar food (like a different shape of pasta).

Understanding these preferences and aversions can help caregivers introduce foods in a way that minimizes anxiety and builds trust. By presenting new foods in a predictable manner or offering them alongside a "safe" food, caregivers can encourage gradual expansion of the individual's diet.

4.5 Nutritional Implications of Restricted Eating

Due to the restrictive nature of these eating challenges, many individuals with ASD are at risk of nutritional deficiencies. A diet limited to a few preferred foods may lack essential vitamins, minerals, and protein, which are vital for growth, development, and overall health.

- **Vitamin and Mineral Deficiencies**: Restrictive diets may lead to deficiencies in critical nutrients like vitamin D, calcium, iron, and essential fatty acids, which can affect physical health, immune function, and cognitive development.
- **Potential Need for Supplements**: For individuals with highly limited diets, dietary supplements may be necessary to meet nutritional requirements. However, introducing supplements can also be challenging if the individual has sensory sensitivities to pills or liquid supplements, making it essential to find acceptable forms of supplementation.
- **Impact on Mental and Physical Well-being**: Poor nutrition can contribute to low energy levels, mood issues, and irritability, which can, in turn, exacerbate ASD symptoms. It is crucial for caregivers and healthcare providers to monitor the individual's nutritional intake closely and address gaps through carefully tailored strategies.

4.6 Strategies for Addressing Sensory-Based and Rigid Eating Challenges

Managing sensory-based and rigid eating challenges requires a combination of patience, creativity, and specialized support. Some approaches include:

- **Gradual Exposure**: Introducing new foods gradually, in small portions, or in a way that respects the individual's sensory needs (e.g., presenting it on a separate plate) can help reduce anxiety and increase acceptance over time.
- **Offering Sensory-Appropriate Alternatives**: Providing similar sensory experiences to favorite foods (e.g., offering freeze-dried fruits to mimic crunchy textures) can expand the diet while meeting sensory needs.
- **Occupational Therapy**: For those with sensory or motor-based challenges, occupational therapy can help build tolerance for different textures and work on oral-motor skills to ease the eating process.
- **Working with a Dietitian**: A registered dietitian can help design a nutrition plan that respects the individual's food preferences while introducing a variety of nutrients, using hidden nutrition techniques, fortified foods, or safe supplements as needed.

4.7 Building a Supportive Eating Environment

Creating a supportive and low-stress eating environment is essential for encouraging individuals with ASD to engage with food positively. This may include:

- **Predictable Mealtime Routines**: Keeping meals at consistent times and in familiar settings can provide comfort and reduce anxiety.
- **Respecting Food Boundaries**: Allowing individuals to have control over what they eat, without pressure, helps build trust and a sense of autonomy. Gentle encouragement to try new foods should respect the individual's comfort level.

- **Positive Reinforcement**: Reinforcing small steps toward trying new foods with positive feedback or rewards can make the experience enjoyable, supporting gradual dietary expansion.

By understanding and working with these eating challenges, caregivers and professionals can create a balanced approach that respects individual needs while supporting nutrition and growth. In the following chapters, we will continue exploring the complexities of eating on the autism spectrum, including therapeutic interventions and tools to support a well-rounded and sustainable approach to eating challenges.

Chapter 5

The Role of Sensory Processing in Eating

Sensory processing is a core component of Autism Spectrum Disorder (ASD) that significantly influences various behaviors, including eating habits. Individuals on the autism spectrum often experience heightened or reduced sensitivity to sensory inputs such as taste, smell, texture, and appearance. These sensitivities affect their food choices, eating routines, and overall dietary habits. In this chapter, we'll explore the impact of sensory processing on eating, highlighting how different sensory responses shape food preferences, create challenges, and influence daily nutritional intake for those with ASD.

5.1 Understanding Sensory Processing and Autism

Sensory processing refers to how the brain interprets information from the five senses—taste, touch, smell, sight, and sound. In individuals with ASD, sensory processing often differs from typical patterns, which can lead to either heightened sensitivity (hypersensitivity) or decreased sensitivity (hyposensitivity) to specific stimuli. These unique sensory profiles directly impact how individuals perceive and interact with food.

In ASD, sensory processing differences can manifest as an aversion to certain food characteristics (like texture or color) or as a strong preference for specific sensory experiences (such as crunchy or cold foods). These responses aren't just matters of preference but are often deep-seated reactions that cause discomfort, stress, or pleasure, affecting their approach to eating in ways that may seem unusual or extreme to others.

5.2 How Texture Sensitivity Impacts Food Choices

Texture sensitivity is among the most common sensory issues affecting individuals with ASD. Many people with autism find certain textures intolerable or irresistible, influencing their willingness to try and enjoy specific foods.

- **Aversion to Certain Textures**: Individuals with texture aversion may avoid foods with a "slimy" or "mushy" feel, such as cooked vegetables, yogurt, or certain fruits like bananas. These foods may provoke gagging, discomfort, or even distress, leading to a strong refusal to eat them.

- **Preference for Specific Textures**: Conversely, some people with ASD may seek out specific textures, like crunchy foods (e.g., crackers, carrots, or chips) because they find the sensation satisfying or soothing. This can lead to a narrow diet focused on a particular texture, limiting exposure to other foods and potentially causing nutritional imbalances.
- **Resistance to Mixed Textures**: Many individuals on the spectrum dislike foods with mixed textures, like soups, casseroles, or layered foods. For them, the unpredictability of encountering different textures in one bite can be overwhelming, leading to avoidance of these types of dishes.

5.3 The Role of Smell in Eating Habits

Smell plays a powerful role in the eating experience, especially for those with heightened olfactory sensitivity. A strong smell can make certain foods appealing or cause a strong aversion, impacting what someone with ASD is willing to eat.

- **Aversion to Strong Smells**: Individuals with ASD often avoid foods with intense odors, like cooked fish, garlic, or certain cheeses. Even the smell of a disliked food being prepared nearby can be overwhelming, leading to complete avoidance of that food or refusal to eat.
- **Preferences for Subtle Smells**: Some individuals prefer foods with mild or no smell, such as plain rice, bread, or certain fruits, as these are less likely to trigger an intense olfactory response. This preference can limit the types of food they feel comfortable trying, reinforcing a narrow eating pattern.
- **Environmental Impact**: The environment in which a meal is served can also influence eating behaviors. The presence of strong food smells in a shared eating space may make individuals with ASD uncomfortable, causing them to eat less or refuse food altogether in environments like school cafeterias or restaurants.

5.4 Taste Sensitivity: Navigating Flavor Preferences and Aversions

Taste sensitivity also affects food choices and can contribute to the development of restrictive eating patterns. Some individuals with ASD may have heightened sensitivity to strong flavors, while others may not register flavors as intensely and instead seek out bold or highly flavored foods.

- **Hypersensitivity to Flavors**: Individuals who are highly sensitive to flavors may avoid foods that are bitter, sour, or strongly flavored, including vegetables like broccoli or foods with complex seasonings. This sensitivity often results in a preference for bland or mildly flavored foods, narrowing dietary options.
- **Hyposensitivity to Flavors**: On the other hand, some people with ASD may have reduced taste sensitivity and seek out bold, strong flavors. This can lead to a preference for spicy, salty, or heavily seasoned foods. Although this doesn't typically limit their diet, it can create unique challenges when the individual's food choices don't align with available options.
- **Impact on Nutritional Intake**: Taste preferences directly influence nutritional intake, as an aversion to bitter or sour flavors, for example, may lead to avoidance of nutrient-rich vegetables, fruits, and certain proteins. Caregivers and professionals often work to create strategies for introducing nutrient-dense foods in a way that aligns with the individual's taste profile.

5.5 Visual Sensitivity and Food Preferences

Visual perception plays a subtle yet crucial role in eating habits, as many individuals with ASD react to the appearance of food, including its color, shape, and presentation.

- **Color Sensitivity**: Some individuals with ASD display color preferences or aversions, where they might refuse foods of a certain color (e.g., green foods) or favor foods of one color, such as only eating beige foods. This sensitivity can limit variety, especially if the aversion includes colorful vegetables or fruits.

- **Need for Predictability in Appearance**: Visual consistency can be essential for some individuals on the autism spectrum. Foods that appear unpredictable or inconsistent (e.g., an apple with a bruise or a salad with mixed colors) may be rejected. This preference for predictability can lead to a narrow selection of foods that meet specific visual criteria.
- **Impact of Presentation**: The way food is arranged or presented on a plate can also affect eating. Many individuals with ASD prefer foods to be separated and may resist mixed dishes or foods that appear "messy." Understanding these visual needs helps caregivers structure meals in a way that encourages eating without discomfort.

5.6 Sound Sensitivity and Mealtime Environment

While less discussed, sound sensitivity can impact eating behaviors, as individuals with ASD may have strong reactions to certain sounds during meals, whether from the food itself or the surrounding environment.

- **Aversion to Eating Sounds**: Crunching, slurping, or chewing sounds can be distressing to individuals with heightened auditory sensitivity. This may cause them to avoid certain foods or eat in isolation to minimize exposure to these sounds.
- **Distractions from Background Noise**: Noisy environments can make mealtimes challenging, as background sounds, such as loud conversations or kitchen noises, may be overwhelming. For those sensitive to sound, eating in a quiet, controlled environment can help reduce sensory overload and create a more comfortable dining experience.

5.7 Strategies for Supporting Sensory-Based Eating Challenges

Addressing sensory sensitivities in eating requires strategies tailored to the individual's unique sensory profile. Here are some effective approaches:

- **Gradual Sensory Exposure**: Introducing new foods gradually, starting with small portions and textures similar to the individual's preferences, can help build tolerance to new sensory experiences over time.
- **Food Preparation Modifications**: Modifying textures (e.g., pureeing vegetables or serving foods in their preferred texture) can make eating more manageable. This helps maintain nutritional diversity without causing sensory distress.
- **Sensory-Appropriate Eating Environments**: Creating a calming and predictable eating environment—such as a quiet dining area with minimal distractions—supports those with auditory and visual sensitivities, making mealtime a more pleasant experience.
- **Involving Occupational Therapists**: Occupational therapists specializing in sensory integration can work with individuals to address sensory aversions and improve tolerance. Techniques may include sensory-based play, texture exploration, and desensitization exercises, helping individuals expand their dietary preferences.

5.8 Supporting Long-Term Sensory and Eating Needs

Understanding and addressing sensory processing in relation to eating is an ongoing process. Each individual's sensory needs may shift over time, and continuous adjustments to food choices, preparation methods, and mealtime environments can support long-term health and well-being. Collaboration with professionals, such as dietitians and occupational therapists, can provide valuable guidance, especially in cases where sensory sensitivities impact nutritional intake.

Moving forward, we'll examine how caregivers and professionals can employ therapeutic approaches and support systems that consider the complex interplay between sensory processing and eating. With these insights, we aim to create a more balanced, individualized approach to nutrition for those on the autism spectrum, fostering both comfort and health in mealtime routines.

Chapter 6: The Psychology of Food Selectivity

Selective eating, often characterized by a strong preference for a limited range of foods, is common among individuals with autism. While sensory sensitivities play a prominent role, there are also emotional and psychological factors that influence food selectivity. In this chapter, we'll explore the psychological aspects that contribute to food preferences, aversions, and eating habits in individuals on the autism spectrum. Understanding these factors offers insight into the deeper emotional connections and anxieties surrounding food and provides pathways for caregivers to support healthier, more varied eating behaviors.

6.1 Defining Food Selectivity in Autism

Food selectivity in autism refers to the preference for or avoidance of specific foods based on sensory, emotional, and cognitive factors. It's often characterized by:
- **Limited Food Variety**: Relying on a small set of foods and rejecting a broader range.
- **Preference for Specific Food Qualities**: Favoring foods with particular textures, colors, flavors, or brands.
- **Routine-Driven Choices**: Preferring certain foods based on familiarity, structure, and predictability.

While many children go through "picky eating" phases, individuals with autism may continue selective eating well into adulthood, impacting their nutrition and health.

6.2 Emotional Responses and Anxiety Around Food

For individuals with autism, food selectivity can be deeply tied to emotions and anxiety. The process of trying new foods or experiencing unexpected textures can provoke intense emotional reactions, including fear and stress.
- **Fear of New Foods (Neophobia)**: Many individuals with autism experience neophobia, or fear of new foods. The unpredictability of trying something unfamiliar can lead to significant anxiety, as new tastes or textures might be overwhelming or unpleasant. For some, even the appearance of new foods on the plate can be distressing.

- **Food as a Source of Comfort**: Certain foods can provide emotional comfort, creating a sense of routine and stability. In moments of stress or sensory overload, familiar foods can offer a calming effect, becoming part of self-soothing behaviors.
- **Anxiety-Driven Control**: Food selectivity can also be a means of exerting control in an unpredictable world. By adhering to a familiar set of foods, individuals with autism may feel a sense of security and control, especially when faced with sensory challenges or changes in routine.

6.3 The Role of Routines and Rituals in Eating

Routine and predictability are often essential for individuals with autism, and this extends to eating habits. Many prefer eating the same foods in the same manner daily, forming rituals that make mealtime more predictable and less stressful.

- **Food Predictability**: Choosing the same food every day or eating in a specific order can create a comforting routine. For instance, eating a peanut butter sandwich for lunch every day reduces the uncertainty of what the taste or texture will be, making mealtime a more stable experience.
- **Preference for Structure**: Food selectivity is often linked to a need for structure. Many individuals may have specific "rules" about how food is arranged on the plate, the utensils used, or the setting in which they eat. Disrupting these rituals can lead to distress or refusal to eat.
- **Building Routine Flexibility**: Although routines offer comfort, overly rigid eating habits can restrict nutrition. Gradual changes, like introducing similar foods to preferred items, can help build flexibility while maintaining a sense of predictability.

6.4 Cognitive and Perceptual Differences in Food Perception

Differences in perception and cognitive processing also influence how people with autism experience food. Cognitive factors, such as literal thinking, difficulty generalizing, and black-and-white thinking, shape how food is interpreted and categorized.

- **Literal Thinking and Food Preferences**: Literal thinking may lead to rigid interpretations of food. For example, if a child tries a food once and dislikes it, they may conclude that "all green foods are bad" or "mushy foods make me feel sick." This black-and-white thinking style can result in the rejection of entire food categories based on a single experience.
- **Difficulty Generalizing**: Many individuals with autism struggle with generalizing experiences. If they enjoy one brand of food, they may only want that specific brand, viewing other similar items as unacceptable. This preference for specific brands or types can limit dietary variety and lead to "brand loyalty" for familiar foods.
- **Visual and Cognitive Consistency**: Cognitive differences also affect how food consistency is perceived. Visual differences, such as a slight color variation or a change in portion size, can disrupt the individual's comfort with a meal. Even minor inconsistencies in food presentation can lead to refusal to eat, as it no longer aligns with their expected experience.

6.5 Sensory Overload and Emotional Eating Responses

The experience of sensory overload can often lead to emotional responses tied to food, influencing selectivity and mealtime behavior. Sensory and psychological factors often work together, amplifying the discomfort associated with certain foods.

- **Sensory-Related Stress and Avoidance**: When faced with foods that provoke sensory discomfort, individuals with autism may experience stress responses, such as increased heart rate or feelings of nausea. Over time, this stress response can create a psychological aversion, where the sight or smell of specific foods triggers negative emotional reactions.
- **Emotional Coping and Food**: Certain foods may become coping mechanisms to handle sensory or emotional stress. "Safe" foods often provide comfort and are easier to digest both physically and emotionally, reinforcing selectivity around these items during times of stress.
- **Negative Associations with Food**: For some, past negative experiences with food, such as choking, gagging, or feeling overwhelmed by a texture, can lead to strong aversions. These associations can create barriers to trying similar foods in the future, as the memory of discomfort overrides the willingness to experiment.

6.6 Social and Environmental Influences on Selective Eating

Eating is also a social experience, and individuals with autism may face unique psychological pressures in social settings that influence food selectivity.

- **Social Anxiety and Eating Preferences**: Social anxiety can make eating around others challenging. For instance, eating in school cafeterias or at social gatherings may lead to food refusal due to anxiety about others watching or commenting on food choices. This can contribute to a preference for solitary meals and familiar foods.
- **Peer Influence and Social Norms**: Social expectations can also reinforce selective eating. Some individuals with autism may feel pressured to adhere to eating patterns that align with family preferences or peer influences. However, because social interactions can feel overwhelming, individuals with autism may gravitate toward selective eating as a form of self-protection in group settings.

- **Environmental Impact on Eating Behavior**: Environmental factors, such as lighting, sounds, and the physical layout of the eating space, also play a role. Eating in a loud, brightly lit cafeteria can be overstimulating and discourage eating, reinforcing selectivity by making meals uncomfortable in such settings.

6.7 Strategies for Addressing Psychological Barriers to Food Diversity

Addressing psychological factors in food selectivity requires supportive strategies that respect the individual's emotional and sensory needs.

- **Building Trust and Predictability**: Creating a safe, predictable mealtime environment helps reduce anxiety. Gradual exposure to new foods without pressure or expectations can build trust, allowing individuals to approach unfamiliar foods at their own pace.
- **Incorporating Food Play**: Playful interactions with food, such as cooking together or engaging in sensory play, can introduce new textures and smells in a low-pressure way. By removing the immediate expectation of eating, food play can foster positive associations with diverse foods.
- **Positive Reinforcement Techniques**: Reinforcing small successes, like tasting a new food without the requirement to eat it fully, can encourage exploration. Positive reinforcement helps create positive emotional connections to new foods, easing anxiety and building comfort.
- **Mindfulness and Emotional Regulation**: Mindfulness techniques can help individuals with autism become more attuned to their bodily responses and emotions around food. Simple exercises, such as breathing techniques or grounding exercises, can reduce anxiety and foster a more relaxed approach to eating.

- **Working with Therapists**: Professionals, including psychologists and occupational therapists, can provide support to address anxiety, neophobia, and other psychological challenges related to eating. Cognitive-behavioral techniques can also help individuals reframe negative associations and build resilience in trying new foods.

6.8 Moving Toward a Balanced Relationship with Food

Developing a healthy relationship with food is a journey that involves both the individual and their support network. By understanding and respecting the emotional and psychological aspects of food selectivity, caregivers can help individuals with autism build a more positive, less stressful approach to eating. This chapter underscores the importance of viewing selective eating as a multifaceted experience and using empathy-driven strategies to foster openness, flexibility, and comfort with food over time.

In the following chapter, we will explore specific interventions and therapies tailored to address the challenges of eating selectivity and sensory aversions, helping individuals with autism expand their food preferences and nutritional intake.

Chapter 7

The Importance of Routine in Eating Habits

Routines play a central role in the lives of many individuals with autism spectrum disorder (ASD), providing a sense of structure and predictability that can reduce anxiety and help navigate daily activities. However, when it comes to eating habits, routines can both support and hinder a balanced diet. Many people with autism develop highly specific eating patterns based on routines that limit food variety and may restrict nutritional intake. This chapter examines the essential role that routines play in the eating habits of those with autism, exploring how structured meals can bring comfort yet also create challenges. We'll look at how caregivers and individuals on the spectrum can work together to gradually introduce flexibility without compromising the benefits that routine provides.

7.1 Understanding the Comfort of Routine in Eating

For individuals with ASD, routines offer a predictable framework that makes daily life more manageable. Predictable eating patterns—such as consistent mealtimes, familiar foods, and specific presentation styles—help reduce the stress and anxiety that can accompany meals.

- **Reducing Anxiety with Consistency**: The structured nature of routines reduces the cognitive load associated with decision-making and sensory experiences. When meals follow a known schedule and include familiar foods, the individual can focus on the experience of eating rather than worry about new tastes, smells, or textures.
- **Creating Safe Spaces for Eating**: Eating the same foods in specific settings can provide a sense of control. Many individuals with autism may have "safe foods" that they eat regularly, which makes the act of eating a comfortable and controlled experience.
- **Predictability and Mealtime Stability**: Mealtime routines extend beyond food choices to encompass the environment, utensils, and sequence of activities. For instance, some individuals may need their food arranged in a particular way or may prefer to use the same bowl, plate, or cup each time. This stability allows them to approach meals with a sense of security.

7.2 The Influence of Routine on Food Selectivity

While routines provide comfort, they can also contribute to restrictive eating patterns. Food selectivity in autism is often closely tied to routines, with specific preferences for textures, colors, brands, and even preparation methods that are adhered to with strict consistency.

- **Routine-Driven Food Choices**: Many individuals with autism prefer a narrow range of foods, as this limits sensory surprises and aligns with familiar routines. This can lead to repetitive consumption of the same items, reducing exposure to varied nutrients and potentially impacting health.
- **Brand Loyalty and Specific Preferences**: Some individuals form preferences for specific brands, shapes, or preparations. For instance, they might only eat a particular brand of chicken nuggets or a specific type of bread. Deviating from these preferences can disrupt their comfort, leading to food refusal.
- **Attachment to Food Appearance and Texture**: Visual consistency is essential for many with autism, as small changes in food color, texture, or shape can create discomfort. Even slight variations in how food is presented—like an apple slice versus a whole apple—can disrupt the eating routine.

7.3 The Challenges of Routine Flexibility

Introducing new foods or changing eating routines can be difficult for individuals with autism, as it challenges the predictability they rely on. Rigid routines may limit their ability to adapt to new environments, eat outside of home, or try different foods when familiar items aren't available.

- **Difficulty in Adjusting to New Foods**: Attempts to introduce new foods may be met with resistance, especially when individuals are accustomed to a specific menu. The thought of eating something new can create stress and even lead to behavioral responses, such as food refusal or withdrawal.

- **Social Implications of Rigidity**: Routines around eating can make social situations challenging. Dining out, attending family gatherings, or eating at school might disrupt established routines, creating stress or a reluctance to participate in group meals.
- **Adaptation and Transition Challenges**: For those with autism, changes to routine are generally best approached slowly and with careful planning. However, unexpected changes—like a food being unavailable—can provoke strong negative reactions, as it breaks their established comfort with the routine.

7.4 Balancing Routine with Dietary Variety

Encouraging flexibility while respecting the need for routine is key to creating a balanced approach to eating for individuals on the spectrum. Building flexibility in routine can help introduce new foods and experiences without overwhelming the individual.

- **Gradual Food Exposure**: Introducing new foods in small, incremental steps can help expand dietary variety. Starting with foods that are similar in texture, color, or flavor to current preferences can make new items feel more familiar and approachable.
- **Creating Visual and Sensory Consistency**: To maintain a sense of stability, new foods can be presented in a way that resembles familiar items. For example, if an individual only eats round foods like pizza or burgers, a caregiver might introduce other round items, like pancakes or veggie patties, to encourage variety without disrupting routine.
- **Structured Flexibility Practices**: Encouraging a "structured choice" approach can introduce an element of control and predictability. For instance, presenting a choice between two similar foods allows the individual to make decisions within a limited, structured framework that doesn't feel overwhelming.

7.5 Role of Caregivers and Strategies for Supporting Routine in Mealtimes

Caregivers play a vital role in maintaining routines while gently encouraging food variety. Through careful planning and patience, caregivers can create strategies that respect the need for routine and address nutritional needs.

- **Establishing Routine-Friendly Mealtime Plans**: For families of individuals with autism, it can be helpful to establish predictable mealtime schedules, including the types of foods offered, the utensils used, and even the seating arrangement. Having a visual schedule or daily checklist can reinforce routine and provide comfort.
- **Incorporating Visual Supports**: Visual tools, like a weekly meal chart, can help outline the foods available each day, providing structure while introducing new items gradually. This approach also helps the individual prepare mentally for upcoming meals and reduce the anxiety of unpredictability.
- **Progressive Desensitization Techniques**: For rigid routines, desensitization can help introduce variety by slowly exposing the individual to new experiences. For example, a new food can be placed on the table during several meals without the expectation to eat it, allowing the individual to grow accustomed to its presence.

7.6 The Benefits of Routine Flexibility for Long-Term Eating Habits

Cultivating some degree of flexibility within routines has long-term benefits, particularly as individuals transition into new environments, such as school or work. This flexibility can reduce anxiety around food availability and support social and nutritional well-being.

- **Adapting to New Environments**: For those transitioning into settings like school cafeterias or social gatherings, flexible eating routines can support smoother integration and greater comfort in different settings. Building gradual adaptability makes these situations less stressful and enables more diverse eating options.

- **Supporting Independence**: Routine flexibility can support greater independence in meal planning and food choices, allowing individuals with autism to expand their menu when needed. This independence is particularly valuable in adulthood, where access to familiar foods might be more limited.
- **Fostering Positive Experiences with New Foods**: By incorporating flexibility within routine, individuals can experience positive associations with food variety, making them more open to trying new items. Positive reinforcement, gentle encouragement, and a non-pressurized approach are essential in creating a balanced eating routine.

7.7 Practical Tips for Expanding Routine Comfort Zones

To successfully integrate more flexibility into eating habits, caregivers and individuals can experiment with practical strategies that honor routines while creating openings for new experiences.

- **Setting Small, Achievable Goals**: Introduce one small change at a time, such as adding a new food item to a meal once a week. Celebrating each small success can create a positive cycle of trying new foods.
- **Involving the Individual in Food Choices**: Encourage individuals to participate in grocery shopping, meal planning, and preparation. This allows them to feel more in control of changes and introduces new foods in a safe, participatory environment.
- **Using Positive Reinforcement**: Offering praise or rewards for trying new foods—even just a small taste—can help create positive associations with flexibility. Rewards can be simple, like a favorite activity after trying a new food.

7.8 Building Toward a Balanced Approach to Food and Routine

Establishing a balanced approach to food and routine is essential for fostering healthy eating habits in individuals with autism. By understanding the role of routine in eating and working toward gentle flexibility, caregivers can support a positive, less restrictive approach to mealtime. This approach nurtures both the need for stability and the value of dietary variety, contributing to long-term health and well-being.
In the next chapter, we'll explore how caregivers and individuals can navigate the challenges of sensory aversions, a significant factor in the eating behaviors of people with autism. By addressing these aversions, we'll build on the concepts of routine flexibility to further support a varied and nutritious diet.

Chapter 8

Medical Implications of Restricted Diets

Restricted diets are common among individuals with autism spectrum disorder (ASD), often due to sensory sensitivities, routines, or specific food preferences. While these eating habits can provide comfort and predictability, they may lead to significant nutritional imbalances over time. This chapter delves into the potential health risks associated with restricted diets, highlighting the importance of addressing these issues to support overall well-being.

8.1 Understanding Nutritional Deficiencies in Restricted Diets

A restricted diet can result in inadequate intake of essential nutrients, impacting physical and mental health. For individuals with ASD, whose eating habits may be narrowly focused on specific foods, these risks are heightened.

- **Common Nutritional Deficiencies**:
    - **Vitamins**: Deficiencies in vitamins such as A, D, and B12 are frequent due to limited consumption of fruits, vegetables, and protein-rich foods.
    - **Minerals**: Calcium, zinc, and iron deficiencies often occur in diets lacking dairy or diverse food sources.
    - **Macronutrient Imbalances**: Over-reliance on carbohydrate-heavy or processed foods can lead to insufficient intake of protein and healthy fats.
- **Impact on Growth and Development**: For children with ASD, restricted diets can interfere with normal growth patterns, potentially leading to stunted growth, weakened immune function, or delayed developmental milestones.

8.2 Physical Health Implications of Restricted Diets

Restricted or unbalanced diets can have long-term consequences for physical health. These include:
- **Weakened Bone Health**: Inadequate calcium and vitamin D intake can lead to weakened bones and an increased risk of fractures. This is particularly concerning during childhood and adolescence, critical periods for bone development.

- **Anemia**: Iron deficiency, common in individuals with restricted diets, can cause fatigue, irritability, and difficulty concentrating. For some, it may lead to more severe forms of anemia requiring medical intervention.
- **Gastrointestinal Issues**: Limited fiber intake, often associated with low consumption of fruits and vegetables, can contribute to constipation, a common concern among individuals with autism.
- **Weakened Immune Function**: Nutrient deficiencies can impair the immune system, making individuals more susceptible to infections and illnesses.

8.3 Cognitive and Behavioral Impacts of Nutritional Deficiencies

Nutrition plays a critical role in brain function, mood regulation, and behavior. For individuals with ASD, nutritional deficiencies may exacerbate existing challenges.

- **Cognitive Effects**:
    - Deficiencies in omega-3 fatty acids, iron, and zinc have been linked to difficulties in attention, memory, and problem-solving.
    - Low levels of vitamin B12 can contribute to neurological issues, including fatigue and poor concentration.
- **Mood and Behavioral Impacts**:
    - Nutritional imbalances can affect serotonin production, potentially exacerbating anxiety, irritability, or mood swings.
    - Hypoglycemia (low blood sugar) caused by an imbalanced diet can lead to behavioral outbursts or meltdowns.

8.4 Long-Term Health Risks

The long-term consequences of restricted diets extend beyond immediate nutritional deficiencies. Chronic imbalances may contribute to severe health conditions, such as:

- **Metabolic Disorders**: Prolonged over-reliance on processed, sugary foods can increase the risk of developing obesity, diabetes, and other metabolic disorders.
- **Heart Disease**: Diets lacking in healthy fats and high in processed foods can lead to elevated cholesterol levels and an increased risk of cardiovascular disease.
- **Chronic Fatigue and Weakness**: Persistent nutrient deficiencies can lead to ongoing fatigue and reduced physical stamina, impacting daily functioning and quality of life.

8.5 Strategies to Address Nutritional Imbalances

To prevent the health risks associated with restricted diets, targeted interventions can help ensure a more balanced intake of nutrients.

- **Nutritional Assessments**: Regular check-ups with a pediatrician, dietitian, or nutritionist can identify potential deficiencies and provide guidance on dietary improvements.
- **Supplementation**:
  - **Vitamins and Minerals**: When dietary changes are not feasible, supplements can bridge nutritional gaps. For example, calcium, iron, or omega-3 supplements may be recommended.
  - **Tailored Approaches**: Supplements should be chosen based on individual needs and under medical supervision to avoid over-supplementation.
- **Gradual Introduction of New Foods**: Caregivers can support dietary expansion by introducing new foods in small, non-threatening ways. For example, blending a small portion of a new vegetable into a preferred dish can encourage acceptance.
- **Meal Planning and Variety**: Structured meal plans that incorporate a range of food groups can ensure balanced nutrition while respecting sensory preferences.

8.6 Supporting Caregivers in Managing Restricted Diets

Caregivers play a crucial role in addressing the medical implications of restricted diets. Providing them with tools and knowledge can empower them to support healthier eating habits.

- **Education and Resources**: Offering information about nutrient-dense foods, meal planning, and cooking techniques can help caregivers manage dietary challenges effectively.
- **Collaboration with Professionals**: Working with healthcare providers and dietitians ensures a comprehensive approach to addressing nutritional needs.
- **Encouraging Patience and Persistence**: Caregivers should be encouraged to approach dietary changes gradually, recognizing that progress may be slow but meaningful.

8.7 Building Toward Sustainable Nutrition

While addressing restricted diets requires time and effort, the benefits of balanced nutrition are profound. Improved physical health, enhanced cognitive function, and better emotional regulation are all achievable outcomes with the right support. By understanding the medical implications of restricted diets and implementing targeted strategies, individuals with ASD and their caregivers can work toward a healthier and more balanced relationship with food. The next chapter will explore strategies to collaborate with healthcare professionals in creating individualized dietary plans that align with sensory and behavioral needs.

Chapter 9

How ARFID and PICA Are Diagnosed

Diagnosing Avoidant/Restrictive Food Intake Disorder (ARFID) and PICA in individuals with autism spectrum disorder (ASD) is a nuanced process. While these eating challenges have well-defined diagnostic criteria, their presentation in autistic individuals often includes unique complexities, such as overlapping symptoms, sensory sensitivities, and communication barriers. This chapter explores the diagnostic criteria for ARFID and PICA, discusses the tools and approaches used by healthcare professionals, and highlights the challenges and considerations involved in evaluating these conditions within the context of ASD.

9.1 Diagnostic Criteria for ARFID

ARFID is formally recognized in the *Diagnostic and Statistical Manual of Mental Disorders, Fifth Edition (DSM-5)*. The diagnosis is based on specific criteria that differentiate ARFID from other eating disorders, such as anorexia nervosa and bulimia nervosa.

- **Key Diagnostic Features**:
    - **Avoidance or Restriction**: Persistent refusal or avoidance of certain foods, often due to sensory sensitivities, fear of choking or vomiting, or lack of interest in eating.
    - **Nutritional Deficiency**: The eating behavior leads to significant nutritional deficiencies, such as low levels of essential vitamins or minerals.
    - **Dependence on Supplements**: Reliance on oral nutritional supplements or tube feeding may be necessary to meet caloric and nutritional needs.
    - **Impairment in Functioning**: The restricted eating behavior disrupts daily life, such as difficulty attending social meals or maintaining adequate energy levels.
- **Exclusions**: ARFID is diagnosed only when the behavior is not explained by:
    - A medical condition or lack of access to food.
    - Another mental health disorder.
    - Body image concerns (common in other eating disorders).

9.2 Diagnostic Criteria for PICA

PICA is also defined in the *DSM-5* and involves the persistent eating of non-nutritive, non-food items. For individuals with autism, PICA can often be tied to sensory exploration or repetitive behaviors.

- **Key Diagnostic Features**:
    - **Non-Food Consumption**: Recurrent ingestion of non-food substances, such as dirt, paper, chalk, soap, or fabric, for at least one month.
    - **Inappropriate for Developmental Level**: The behavior is considered abnormal for the individual's age or developmental stage.
    - **Not Cultural or Socially Normative**: The behavior is not part of a culturally sanctioned practice.
    - **Impairment or Risk**: The behavior may lead to medical complications, such as gastrointestinal blockages, poisoning, or infections.
- **Exclusions**: Similar to ARFID, PICA is not diagnosed if the behavior is better explained by:
    - Another medical condition, such as iron deficiency anemia, which may cause cravings for non-food substances.
    - A broader mental health condition without specific emphasis on the behavior.

9.3 Tools and Approaches for Diagnosis

Diagnosing ARFID and PICA involves a multi-step evaluation process led by healthcare professionals, including pediatricians, psychologists, and dietitians. The following tools and approaches are commonly used:

- **Clinical Interviews**:
    - A detailed history of eating behaviors, focusing on the duration, frequency, and triggers of the eating challenges.
    - Questions about sensory sensitivities, aversions, and environmental factors influencing eating patterns.

- o Exploration of medical history to rule out underlying health conditions.
- **Behavioral Observations**:
  - o Monitoring the individual during meals to assess food preferences, aversions, and eating behaviors.
  - o Identifying signs of distress, rigidity, or anxiety related to food or mealtimes.
- **Nutritional Assessments**:
  - o Evaluation of growth patterns, weight trends, and nutritional intake to identify deficiencies.
  - o Blood tests to check for anemia, vitamin deficiencies, or other markers of poor nutrition.
- **Psychological Assessments**:
  - o Screening for co-occurring mental health conditions, such as anxiety or obsessive-compulsive disorder (OCD), that might influence eating behaviors.
  - o Use of standardized tools like the Eating Disorder Examination (EDE) or questionnaires tailored to sensory and feeding challenges.
- **Sensory Profiles**:
  - o Assessment of sensory processing issues that may contribute to food avoidance or preferences for non-food items.
  - o Tools like the Sensory Profile Questionnaire can help identify sensitivities to textures, smells, or tastes.

9.4 Challenges in Diagnosing ARFID and PICA in ASD

Diagnosing ARFID and PICA in autistic individuals can be complex, as their eating behaviors often overlap with characteristics of autism itself.
- **Overlap with ASD Traits**:
  - o Many autistic individuals exhibit sensory sensitivities or rigid routines around food, which are hallmarks of ARFID but may not meet the full criteria for the disorder.
  - o Similarly, exploratory or repetitive behaviors in autism, such as mouthing objects, can resemble PICA but may not indicate a true eating disorder.

- **Communication Barriers**:
    - Difficulties in expressing discomfort, fear, or preferences can complicate the diagnostic process, particularly for nonverbal individuals or those with limited verbal communication.
- **Cultural and Environmental Factors**:
    - Limited access to diverse foods, cultural norms around eating, or unstructured mealtime environments can obscure the true nature of the eating behavior.
- **Comorbid Conditions**:
    - Co-occurring conditions, such as anxiety, ADHD, or gastrointestinal disorders, can influence eating habits and make it harder to pinpoint ARFID or PICA as the primary concern.

9.5 The Role of Early Identification and Intervention

Early diagnosis is essential to prevent the medical and psychological complications associated with ARFID and PICA. Proactive screening during routine healthcare visits can help identify at-risk individuals and initiate interventions.

- **The Importance of Early Signs**:
    - Noticing early signs, such as severe food selectivity or persistent ingestion of non-food items, allows for timely referrals to specialists.
    - Addressing eating challenges early can mitigate long-term nutritional deficiencies and reduce the risk of medical complications.
- **Collaboration Across Disciplines**:
    - Effective diagnosis requires collaboration among pediatricians, dietitians, occupational therapists, and behavioral therapists to provide a comprehensive evaluation.
- **Parental and Caregiver Input**:
    - Caregivers offer invaluable insights into the individual's eating behaviors, routines, and sensory preferences. Their observations can guide the diagnostic process and ensure a holistic understanding of the individual's needs.

9.6 Moving Toward Comprehensive Support

Accurate diagnosis of ARFID and PICA is the first step toward developing tailored interventions that address both the individual's eating challenges and their broader needs as someone with ASD. By understanding the diagnostic process and the unique considerations for autistic individuals, caregivers and professionals can work together to support healthier eating habits and improve overall well-being.
In the next chapter, we will explore strategies for addressing sensory aversions, which are a significant factor in many eating challenges faced by individuals with autism. By tackling these sensory sensitivities, we can pave the way for more varied and balanced eating behaviors.

Chapter 10

Signs and Symptoms of Eating Challenges in ASD

Eating challenges are a prevalent issue for individuals with autism spectrum disorder (ASD), manifesting in behaviors and patterns that can vary widely from one person to another. Recognizing the signs and symptoms is crucial for early intervention, as these challenges often have significant implications for physical health, emotional well-being, and overall quality of life. This chapter examines the behavioral, sensory, and physical indicators of eating difficulties commonly observed in individuals with ASD.

10.1 Behavioral Indicators of Eating Challenges

Individuals with ASD often display distinct behaviors around food, driven by sensory sensitivities, routine preferences, or anxiety. These behaviors can serve as early signs of underlying eating difficulties:
- **Severe Food Selectivity**:
    - Preference for a very limited range of foods, often based on color, texture, or brand.
    - Refusal to eat foods that deviate from their preferred options, even if nutritionally necessary.
- **Anxiety Around Mealtimes**:
    - Resistance to sitting at the table or engaging in family meals.
    - Displaying visible distress, such as crying, tantrums, or withdrawal, when presented with unfamiliar or disliked foods.
- **Avoidance of Entire Food Groups**:
    - Omitting categories such as fruits, vegetables, or proteins entirely from their diet.
    - Developing rigid "rules" about acceptable foods, such as only eating crunchy or soft items.
- **Unusual Eating Rituals**:
    - Requiring food to be arranged in a specific way on the plate.
    - Eating foods in a fixed sequence or avoiding foods that touch each other.

10.2 Sensory Symptoms in Eating Challenges

Sensory sensitivities are a hallmark of ASD and play a major role in food preferences and aversions. Sensory processing differences can affect how individuals perceive the taste, texture, smell, and appearance of food.

- **Texture Sensitivities**:
    - Avoidance of foods that are perceived as too mushy, crunchy, slimy, or gritty.
    - Strong preference for specific textures, such as only eating smooth or crunchy foods.
- **Taste and Smell Sensitivities**:
    - Aversion to foods with strong flavors, such as spicy, sour, or bitter tastes.
    - Refusal to eat foods with strong or unfamiliar smells, even if others consider the smell mild.
- **Visual Preferences**:
    - Avoiding foods of a certain color or shape, such as only eating white or round foods.
    - Refusal to eat if the food's appearance is altered (e.g., slightly burnt or inconsistently sized).

10.3 Physical Symptoms of Eating Challenges

Restricted or unbalanced eating patterns can lead to observable physical symptoms that indicate nutritional deficiencies or health issues. These include:

- **Weight Changes**:
    - Sudden weight loss or inability to gain weight, often due to limited calorie intake.
    - Excessive weight gain, particularly if the diet relies heavily on processed or carbohydrate-rich foods.
- **Gastrointestinal Issues**:
    - Frequent complaints of stomach pain, constipation, or diarrhea, which may result from limited fiber intake or food intolerances.
    - Persistent bloating or discomfort after meals.
- **Fatigue and Weakness**:
    - Low energy levels or physical weakness, often due to inadequate protein, iron, or vitamin intake.

- - Difficulty concentrating or staying active during the
      day.
  - **Skin, Hair, and Nail Changes**:
    - Dry or flaky skin, brittle nails, or hair thinning,
      which can signal deficiencies in essential nutrients
      such as zinc or vitamin A.

10.4 Emotional and Social Symptoms

Eating challenges in ASD can also have emotional and social
repercussions, as food and mealtime dynamics are often tied to
social interactions and routines.

- **Food-Related Anxiety**:
  - Worrying about the availability of preferred foods
    in new or unfamiliar settings.
  - Fear of trying new foods (food neophobia) leading
    to heightened stress during meals.
- **Social Withdrawal**:
  - Avoiding social events that involve food, such as
    birthday parties or family gatherings.
  - Feeling isolated from peers due to differences in
    eating habits or preferences.
- **Emotional Outbursts**:
  - Displaying frustration, anger, or sadness when
    food expectations are unmet.
  - Meltdowns triggered by changes in mealtime
    routines or the presence of disliked foods.

10.5 Patterns Unique to ARFID and PICA

While eating challenges in ASD can be broad, certain behaviors
are particularly indicative of specific conditions like ARFID and
PICA:

- **ARFID**:
  - Extreme aversion to eating a variety of foods,
    often tied to sensory processing issues or
    traumatic experiences such as choking.
  - Heavy reliance on nutritional supplements or
    medical interventions to meet dietary needs.
- **PICA**:

- o Persistent consumption of non-food items such as dirt, paper, or fabric, often linked to sensory exploration or underlying nutrient deficiencies.
- o Risk of medical complications such as intestinal blockages or poisoning.

10.6 Observing Signs Across Developmental Stages

Eating challenges may evolve with age, making it essential to monitor symptoms at different developmental stages:
- **Early Childhood**:
  - o Early signs of food selectivity or refusal to transition from breast milk/formula to solid foods.
  - o Difficulty accepting new textures or food types during the weaning process.
- **School-Age Children**:
  - o Increased rigidity around food preferences as routines and preferences become more ingrained.
  - o Social challenges during lunchtime at school, such as refusal to eat or reliance on packed foods.
- **Adolescents and Adults**:
  - o Continued food selectivity that limits social and independent living skills.
  - o Heightened risks of health complications from years of restricted or unbalanced eating.

10.7 The Role of Caregivers and Professionals

Caregivers are often the first to notice signs of eating challenges in individuals with ASD. Their observations, combined with insights from professionals, are key to identifying and addressing these issues.
- **Caregiver Observations**:
  - o Keeping a food diary to track eating behaviors, preferences, and aversions.
  - o Noting physical symptoms like changes in weight, energy levels, or digestion.
- **Professional Assessments**:
  - o Consulting pediatricians, dietitians, or feeding therapists for a comprehensive evaluation.

- o Using sensory profiles and behavioral observations to pinpoint triggers and challenges.

10.8 Building Awareness and Taking Action

Recognizing the signs and symptoms of eating challenges in ASD is the first step toward developing effective strategies for intervention. Early identification allows for tailored approaches that address sensory sensitivities, nutritional needs, and emotional well-being.
The next chapter will delve into the role of caregivers and professionals in creating a supportive environment to foster healthier eating behaviors. By understanding these challenges and working collaboratively, we can help individuals with ASD build a positive and sustainable relationship with food.

Chapter 11

The Role of Healthcare Professionals

Managing eating challenges in autistic individuals, including ARFID, PICA, and other related issues, often requires a multidisciplinary approach. Healthcare professionals play a critical role in diagnosing, addressing, and supporting these challenges, offering expertise that spans nutrition, sensory processing, behavioral health, and overall medical care. This chapter highlights the key professionals involved, their roles in treatment, and how they collaborate to create a comprehensive support system.

11.1 Pediatricians and Primary Care Physicians

Pediatricians or primary care physicians are often the first point of contact for identifying eating challenges. They provide initial assessments and coordinate referrals to specialists.

- **Role in Diagnosis**:
  - Monitoring growth patterns, weight, and nutritional status.
  - Identifying potential medical causes of eating challenges, such as gastrointestinal issues or nutrient deficiencies.
  - Conducting preliminary screenings for ARFID, PICA, or sensory-related eating difficulties.
- **Referral to Specialists**:
  - Directing families to dietitians, occupational therapists, psychologists, or feeding clinics.
  - Ordering laboratory tests to assess for anemia, vitamin deficiencies, or signs of malnutrition.

11.2 Dietitians and Nutritionists

Dietitians and nutritionists specialize in addressing the dietary needs of individuals with restricted or unusual eating behaviors.

- **Assessment and Planning**:
  - Evaluating the individual's current diet to identify deficiencies and risks.
  - Developing personalized meal plans that accommodate sensory preferences while improving nutritional balance.
  - Suggesting safe and palatable ways to introduce new foods into the diet gradually.

- **Nutritional Education**:
  - Guiding caregivers on how to create balanced meals that align with the individual's preferences.
  - Offering alternatives to supplements or processed foods when possible.
- **Monitoring Progress**:
  - Tracking improvements in diet diversity and nutritional status over time.
  - Adjusting plans based on the individual's evolving preferences and needs.

11.3 Occupational Therapists

Occupational therapists (OTs) focus on sensory integration and motor skills related to eating and mealtimes.

- **Addressing Sensory Challenges**:
  - Using sensory integration therapy to help individuals tolerate different textures, smells, and tastes.
  - Introducing gradual desensitization techniques to reduce food aversions.
- **Improving Mealtime Skills**:
  - Supporting motor skills needed for self-feeding, such as holding utensils or chewing effectively.
  - Teaching strategies for managing anxiety or overstimulation during meals.
- **Creating Supportive Environments**:
  - Advising families on how to structure mealtimes to reduce stress and encourage participation.
  - Recommending adaptive tools, such as specialized utensils or seating arrangements, to improve comfort and independence.

11.4 Psychologists and Psychiatrists

Psychologists and psychiatrists address the emotional and behavioral aspects of eating challenges, particularly when anxiety, phobias, or compulsive behaviors are involved.

- **Behavioral Therapy**:

- o Psychologists often use cognitive-behavioral therapy (CBT) to help individuals manage anxiety or negative associations with food.
  - o Applied behavior analysis (ABA) can be used to reinforce positive eating behaviors and reduce avoidance.
- **Addressing Underlying Mental Health Conditions**:
  - o Psychiatrists can diagnose and treat co-occurring conditions, such as anxiety, depression, or OCD, that may exacerbate eating challenges.
  - o In some cases, medication may be prescribed to manage severe anxiety or impulsivity related to eating.
- **Family Counseling**:
  - o Providing support and guidance to caregivers to help them manage the emotional toll of mealtime struggles.
  - o Teaching strategies to create positive mealtime experiences and reduce conflict.

11.5 Speech-Language Pathologists

Speech-language pathologists (SLPs) are instrumental when eating challenges intersect with oral-motor skills or communication barriers.

- **Oral-Motor Skills**:
  - o Assessing and improving chewing, swallowing, and other oral-motor functions necessary for safe and effective eating.
  - o Addressing difficulties such as tongue thrust or poor jaw stability.
- **Communication Support**:
  - o Helping individuals express food preferences, discomfort, or needs, especially for those who are nonverbal.
  - o Teaching caregivers to recognize nonverbal cues related to eating preferences or distress.

11.6 Feeding Therapists

Feeding therapists, who may come from backgrounds in occupational therapy, speech therapy, or psychology, specialize in addressing complex feeding issues.

- **Comprehensive Feeding Assessments**:
  - Evaluating physical, sensory, and emotional factors contributing to feeding difficulties.
  - Observing mealtime behaviors to identify triggers or patterns.
- **Therapeutic Techniques**:
  - Using play-based or exposure therapies to encourage exploration of new foods in a non-threatening way.
  - Implementing structured programs to expand food acceptance gradually.

11.7 Gastroenterologists and Medical Specialists

For individuals with medical complications linked to eating challenges, gastroenterologists and other specialists provide targeted care.

- **Medical Evaluations**:
  - Diagnosing and treating gastrointestinal issues, such as reflux, constipation, or swallowing disorders, that may exacerbate feeding challenges.
  - Investigating and managing potential causes of PICA, such as iron deficiency anemia.
- **Medical Interventions**:
  - Recommending nutritional supplements, tube feeding, or other interventions when oral intake is insufficient.
  - Monitoring and addressing risks associated with eating non-food items, such as intestinal blockages.

11.8 Collaborative Care

Effective management of eating challenges in ASD often requires a team-based approach. Collaboration among healthcare professionals ensures a holistic treatment plan tailored to the individual's unique needs.

- **Interdisciplinary Teams**:
  - Feeding clinics and specialized programs often bring together dietitians, OTs, SLPs, and psychologists to provide integrated care.
  - Regular team meetings and progress updates help align goals and adjust interventions as needed.
- **Caregiver Involvement**:
  - Families are vital partners in the treatment process, providing insights and implementing strategies at home.
  - Professionals work closely with caregivers to ensure consistency and reinforce progress outside of clinical settings.

11.9 Advocating for Comprehensive Support

Healthcare professionals play a pivotal role in advocating for the needs of individuals with ASD and eating challenges. By fostering collaboration, offering education, and addressing barriers to care, they help individuals and families navigate these complex issues and achieve better outcomes.

In the next chapter, we'll explore the importance of caregiver support and strategies for empowering families to manage eating challenges effectively. By working together, professionals and caregivers can create a foundation for positive change and improved quality of life.

Chapter 12

Parent and Caregiver Observations in Diagnosis

Parents and caregivers are often the first to notice changes or challenges in a child's eating habits, especially in children with autism spectrum disorder (ASD). Their close daily interactions offer valuable insights into behaviors, preferences, and patterns that healthcare professionals might not observe in clinical settings. This chapter delves into how these observations can aid in the early identification of eating disorders like ARFID and PICA and outlines the importance of caregiver involvement in the diagnostic process.

12.1 The Vital Role of Caregivers in Diagnosis

Caregivers are uniquely positioned to observe day-to-day eating habits and identify subtle signs of potential problems.

- **Early Recognition of Patterns**:
    - Spotting unusual or restrictive eating behaviors, such as avoiding entire food groups or preferring foods of a specific color or texture.
    - Noting significant shifts in appetite, eating habits, or tolerance for new foods over time.
- **Continuous Monitoring**:
    - Tracking food intake over days, weeks, or months to identify persistent issues.
    - Observing changes during different life stages, such as transitions to solid foods, school settings, or adolescence.
- **Understanding Context**:
    - Providing context about the family's eating environment, cultural practices, and routines that may influence the child's eating behaviors.

12.2 Signs to Look For

Caregivers should be aware of specific behaviors and symptoms that may indicate an eating challenge.

- **Behavioral Signs**:
    - Refusal to eat certain foods or meals, leading to reliance on a narrow range of "safe" foods.
    - Avoidance of social eating situations, such as school lunchrooms or family dinners.

- o Emotional distress, such as crying or tantrums, when offered unfamiliar or disliked foods.
- **Physical Signs**:
  - o Significant weight loss, weight gain, or stagnation in growth.
  - o Complaints of frequent stomachaches, constipation, or other gastrointestinal issues.
  - o Visible signs of malnutrition, such as dry skin, hair loss, or brittle nails.
- **Sensory Triggers**:
  - o Extreme sensitivity to food textures, smells, or appearances.
  - o Strong aversions to certain temperatures, such as refusing warm or cold foods.
- **Unusual Behaviors**:
  - o Persistent consumption of non-food items (indicative of PICA), such as dirt, paper, or chalk.
  - o Development of rigid rituals, like needing food arranged in a specific way on the plate.

12.3 Tools and Strategies for Effective Observation

Parents and caregivers can use structured approaches to monitor eating behaviors and gather data to share with healthcare professionals.

- **Food Diaries**:
  - o Keeping a detailed log of meals, snacks, and beverages consumed, including quantities and types of foods.
  - o Recording reactions to different foods, including refusal, acceptance, or physical symptoms like bloating or pain.
- **Behavioral Logs**:
  - o Documenting the child's mood, energy levels, and behaviors during and after meals.
  - o Noting external factors, such as mealtime environment or stressors, that might influence eating habits.
- **Sensory Assessments**:
  - o Tracking responses to various textures, flavors, and smells to identify patterns or triggers.

- Using questionnaires or sensory profiles designed for children with ASD.

12.4 Communicating Observations to Professionals

Clear communication between caregivers and healthcare providers is essential for accurate diagnosis and effective treatment.
- **Providing Detailed Histories**:
    - Sharing comprehensive accounts of eating habits, sensory sensitivities, and mealtime dynamics.
    - Highlighting significant milestones or changes, such as the onset of food refusal or new preferences.
- **Using Visual Aids**:
    - Bringing photos or samples of preferred and refused foods to appointments.
    - Presenting data from food diaries or behavioral logs in an organized manner.
- **Advocating for Concerns**:
    - Emphasizing the impact of eating challenges on the individual's health, mood, or social interactions.
    - Asking questions to ensure that concerns are thoroughly explored during medical evaluations.

12.5 Case Study: A Caregiver's Perspective

Amanda, a mother of a seven-year-old boy with ASD, noticed that her son, Ethan, would only eat crunchy, beige-colored foods like crackers and chicken nuggets. Over time, she realized Ethan refused all fruits and vegetables, even when disguised in other dishes. Amanda began keeping a food diary, which revealed that Ethan's diet lacked essential nutrients. She also documented his tantrums when presented with new foods and his anxiety during family meals. Armed with this information, Amanda consulted a pediatrician and a dietitian, who diagnosed Ethan with ARFID and developed a tailored treatment plan.
This example underscores how a caregiver's detailed observations can significantly aid in diagnosing eating challenges and setting the stage for intervention.

12.6 Challenges Caregivers May Face

Despite their critical role, caregivers often encounter obstacles when monitoring and reporting eating behaviors.

- **Emotional Toll**:
  - Dealing with the stress and guilt of navigating mealtime struggles.
  - Balancing the needs of the individual with those of other family members.
- **Navigating Biases**:
  - Overcoming misconceptions that selective eating is merely a phase or a lack of discipline.
  - Advocating for a thorough evaluation when professionals dismiss concerns.
- **Time Constraints**:
  - Finding the time to document behaviors and manage appointments with specialists.
  - Balancing observation efforts with work, caregiving, and other responsibilities.

12.7 Supporting Caregivers In Their Role

Healthcare professionals and support networks can empower caregivers by offering tools, education, and encouragement.

- **Education and Training**:
  - Providing resources on sensory sensitivities, common eating disorders, and effective observation techniques.
  - Teaching caregivers how to identify and respond to early warning signs.
- **Peer Support**:
  - Connecting caregivers with support groups or communities where they can share experiences and strategies.
  - Offering counseling or emotional support for those struggling with the demands of caregiving.
- **Professional Collaboration**:
  - Encouraging regular communication between caregivers and multidisciplinary teams to align goals and strategies.

- o Valuing caregivers as integral partners in the diagnostic and treatment process.

12.8 The Caregiver's Impact on Outcomes

Caregivers who are actively involved in monitoring and addressing eating challenges can significantly improve outcomes for individuals with ASD. Their detailed observations and commitment to seeking help provide the foundation for effective intervention.

In the next chapter, we will explore the various therapeutic approaches available for managing eating challenges, highlighting the roles of behavioral, sensory, and nutritional therapies. Together, these strategies aim to create a holistic path toward better health and well-being.

Chapter 13

Screening Tools and Questionnaires

Effective identification of eating challenges in individuals with autism spectrum disorder (ASD) requires the use of reliable and validated screening tools. These tools help healthcare professionals, caregivers, and educators assess the severity, underlying causes, and potential impacts of eating behaviors, paving the way for accurate diagnosis and targeted intervention. This chapter provides an overview of commonly used screening tools, questionnaires, and assessment methods for evaluating eating challenges such as ARFID, PICA, and other feeding issues on the spectrum.

13.1 The Importance of Screening Tools

Screening tools and questionnaires serve as the first step in identifying potential eating disorders or challenges.
- **Key Objectives**:
    - Detect early signs of eating difficulties before they escalate into severe issues.
    - Differentiate between typical developmental phases and clinically significant disorders.
    - Identify co-occurring factors, such as sensory sensitivities or anxiety, that contribute to eating challenges.
- **Advantages of Structured Tools**:
    - Provide standardized criteria for comparison across individuals.
    - Facilitate communication between caregivers and professionals by offering a clear framework.
    - Aid in creating a baseline for monitoring progress during interventions.

13.2 Tools for Screening Eating Challenges

Several tools are specifically designed to assess feeding and eating issues in individuals with ASD or related conditions.

1. Behavioral Pediatrics Feeding Assessment Scale (BPFAS)
- **Purpose**: Evaluates mealtime behaviors and feeding challenges in children.

- **Structure**: A caregiver-completed questionnaire assessing 35 feeding-related behaviors, including food refusal, tantrums, and mealtime disruptions.
- **Application**: Identifies patterns of feeding difficulties and helps distinguish between behavioral and sensory-driven issues.

2. Children's Eating Behavior Questionnaire (CEBQ)
- **Purpose**: Measures eating styles and tendencies in children, such as food responsiveness, enjoyment of food, and emotional under-eating.
- **Structure**: A 35-item caregiver-completed tool that provides insights into a child's relationship with food.
- **Application**: Useful for assessing food selectivity and identifying potential ARFID symptoms.

3. Sensory Processing and Eating Checklist
- **Purpose**: Assesses sensory contributions to feeding difficulties.
- **Structure**: A checklist that evaluates reactions to food textures, temperatures, smells, and other sensory factors.
- **Application**: Helps identify sensory sensitivities that may underlie selective eating or food refusal.

4. The PICA Inventory
- **Purpose**: Screens for behaviors associated with PICA, including the types and frequency of non-food items consumed.
- **Structure**: Caregiver-reported inventory that documents occurrences and potential triggers for PICA-related behaviors.
- **Application**: Assists in diagnosing PICA and developing strategies to address the behavior safely.

5. Screening Tool of Feeding Problems (STEP)
- **Purpose**: Evaluates the presence and severity of feeding problems.
- **Structure**: A structured caregiver interview focusing on mealtime behaviors, food preferences, and aversions.

- **Application**: Identifies feeding challenges specific to individuals with developmental disorders.

13.3 General Tools for ASD and Co-Occurring Conditions

Eating difficulties often overlap with broader challenges in ASD, such as sensory sensitivities, anxiety, or communication barriers. General ASD assessment tools can complement specific feeding evaluations.

1. Autism Diagnostic Observation Schedule (ADOS)
- **Purpose**: A gold-standard tool for diagnosing autism, which includes observations related to restricted or repetitive behaviors, including eating habits.
- **Application**: Provides context for how eating challenges fit within the broader framework of ASD symptoms.

2. Sensory Profile 2
- **Purpose**: Evaluates sensory processing patterns in children and their impact on daily activities, including eating.
- **Structure**: Caregiver-reported questionnaire assessing sensory preferences and aversions.
- **Application**: Identifies how sensory sensitivities influence food choices and mealtime behaviors.

3. Vineland Adaptive Behavior Scales (VABS)
- **Purpose**: Measures adaptive behaviors, including eating and self-care, in individuals with developmental disorders.
- **Application**: Assesses mealtime independence and identifies areas requiring support or intervention.

13.4 Custom Questionnaires and Observational Tools

In addition to standardized tools, custom questionnaires and observational checklists can be tailored to the individual's unique needs and circumstances.
- **Custom Food Logs**:
  - Caregivers record detailed information about food intake, preferences, and aversions.

- o Professionals analyze these logs to identify patterns and triggers.
- **Mealtime Observations**:
  - o Professionals observe the individual during meals to evaluate motor skills, sensory responses, and interactions with food.
  - o Insights from these observations inform personalized intervention strategies.
- **Dietary Recall Interviews**:
  - o Structured interviews with caregivers or individuals to document typical eating habits and challenges.
  - o Useful for gathering qualitative data about emotional and environmental factors influencing eating.

13.5 Challenges in Screening

Despite their value, screening tools have limitations and may require careful interpretation.
- **Caregiver Bias**:
  - o Responses may be influenced by caregivers' perceptions, leading to over- or under-reporting of issues.
- **Cultural Considerations**:
  - o Food preferences and mealtime behaviors vary across cultures, which can affect the interpretation of results.
- **Overlap with Other Conditions**:
  - o Feeding difficulties may stem from co-occurring conditions, such as anxiety or gastrointestinal disorders, complicating the diagnostic process.

13.6 Integrating Screening Results into Care Plans

The data gathered from screening tools and questionnaires guide the development of personalized care plans.
- **Collaborative Analysis**:
  - o Professionals review results with caregivers to identify priorities and set goals.
- **Targeted Interventions**:

- o Screening results inform the selection of therapies, such as sensory integration, behavioral therapy, or dietary counseling.
- **Monitoring Progress**:
  - o Repeated use of tools over time helps track improvements and adjust strategies.

13.7 Empowering Caregivers Through Screening

Providing caregivers with tools to observe and document eating behaviors empowers them to actively participate in the diagnostic process. When caregivers understand the purpose and value of screening tools, they are better equipped to advocate for appropriate interventions.

In the next chapter, we'll delve into therapeutic approaches for managing eating challenges, focusing on strategies tailored to the unique needs of individuals on the autism spectrum. Through therapy, individuals and their caregivers can build healthier and more positive relationships with food.

Chapter 14

Medical Tests and Nutritional Assessments

Eating challenges in individuals on the autism spectrum often lead to concerns about nutritional deficiencies, underlying health issues, or complications caused by restrictive diets. This chapter provides an overview of the medical tests and nutritional assessments used to evaluate overall health, identify deficiencies, and inform intervention strategies.

14.1 The Need for Medical Testing

Restricted eating habits or behaviors like ARFID and PICA can lead to significant health risks, including:
- **Nutritional Deficiencies**:
  - Lack of essential vitamins and minerals due to limited food variety.
  - Low intake of protein, fiber, or healthy fats critical for growth and development.
- **Gastrointestinal Issues**:
  - Problems like constipation, acid reflux, or stomach pain due to unbalanced diets.
  - Conditions such as celiac disease or food intolerances that may exacerbate eating challenges.
- **PICA-Related Risks**:
  - Exposure to toxins or physical damage to the digestive tract from consuming non-food items.

Medical testing is crucial for identifying these underlying issues and preventing long-term complications.

14.2 Common Medical Tests for Eating Challenges

Several medical tests are often recommended to assess health in individuals with eating disorders or challenges:

1. Blood Tests

Bloodwork provides a comprehensive look at nutritional status and overall health:
- **Complete Blood Count (CBC)**: Detects anemia, infections, or other abnormalities.
- **Iron Studies**: Evaluates iron levels to diagnose anemia, common in restrictive diets or PICA.
- **Vitamin Levels**: Assesses levels of vitamins such as B12, D, and folate.

- **Mineral Levels**: Measures critical minerals like calcium, magnesium, and zinc.

2. Metabolic Panel
- **Purpose**: Evaluates kidney and liver function, electrolyte balance, and glucose levels.
- **Application**: Detects imbalances caused by poor nutrition or dehydration.

3. Thyroid Function Tests
- **Purpose**: Measures thyroid hormone levels to rule out thyroid-related metabolic issues.
- **Application**: Addresses unexplained weight changes or fatigue related to eating challenges.

4. Gastrointestinal Testing
Restricted diets can lead to or exacerbate GI problems, requiring further investigation:
- **Lactose Intolerance Test**: Identifies difficulty digesting lactose, a common trigger for food avoidance.
- **Celiac Disease Screening**: Detects gluten intolerance, which can cause abdominal pain and nutrient malabsorption.
- **Stool Tests**: Screens for infections, inflammation, or malabsorption issues.

5. Toxicology Screen for PICA
- **Purpose**: Identifies exposure to toxins such as lead, mercury, or other harmful substances.
- **Application**: Particularly important for individuals exhibiting PICA behaviors.

14.3 Nutritional Assessments

Nutritional assessments help determine dietary gaps and guide personalized intervention strategies.
1. Dietary Intake Analysis
- **Purpose**: Provides a snapshot of daily calorie and nutrient consumption.
- **Method**:

- o Caregivers or individuals track food intake over several days.
  - o Professionals analyze the data to identify deficiencies or excesses.

2. Anthropometric Measurements

- **Purpose**: Evaluates growth and body composition to assess nutritional status.
- **Key Metrics**:
  - o Height, weight, and body mass index (BMI).
  - o Head circumference for younger children.
  - o Skinfold thickness or other measures of body fat.

3. Bone Density Testing

- **Purpose**: Screens for bone health in individuals with long-term calcium or vitamin D deficiencies.
- **Application**: Particularly relevant for individuals who avoid dairy products or exhibit limited outdoor activity.

4. Food Sensitivity and Allergy Testing

- **Purpose**: Identifies potential food allergies or sensitivities that may trigger aversions or health issues.
- **Tests**:
  - o Skin prick tests or blood tests for IgE antibodies.
  - o Elimination diets under medical supervision.

14.4 Interpreting Test Results

Once test results are available, professionals collaborate to create a clear picture of the individual's health and nutritional needs:

- **Holistic Analysis**: Integrating medical, sensory, and behavioral data to understand the root causes of eating challenges.
- **Personalized Recommendations**: Developing dietary plans or interventions tailored to the individual's preferences, sensory needs, and health goals.

14.5 Challenges and Considerations

- **Testing Accessibility**:
    - Some families may face challenges accessing specialized tests due to cost or location.
    - Advocacy and financial assistance programs can help address these barriers.
- **Cooperation in Testing**:
    - Medical tests, especially bloodwork, may be stressful for individuals with ASD due to sensory sensitivities or anxiety.
    - Strategies like social stories, calming techniques, or sedation may be necessary for a smooth process.
- **Overlapping Diagnoses**:
    - Interpreting results can be complex in individuals with co-occurring conditions, requiring multidisciplinary collaboration.

14.6 Building a Care Team

A comprehensive evaluation often involves input from a team of professionals, including:
- **Pediatricians and Primary Care Physicians**: Coordinate initial testing and referrals.
- **Dietitians and Nutritionists**: Provide expertise in dietary assessments and meal planning.
- **Gastroenterologists**: Address GI-specific issues related to restricted diets or PICA.
- **Endocrinologists**: Investigate hormonal imbalances affecting metabolism or growth.

14.7 Supporting Families During Testing

Medical and nutritional assessments can be overwhelming for families. Support strategies include:
- **Clear Communication**: Explaining the purpose and process of each test to caregivers and individuals.
- **Emotional Support**: Offering counseling or support groups to address anxiety or stress related to medical evaluations.

- **Actionable Guidance**: Providing follow-up resources and clear next steps after test results are shared.

14.8 Conclusion

Medical tests and nutritional assessments are crucial for understanding the impact of eating challenges on the health of individuals with ASD. By identifying underlying issues and guiding targeted interventions, these evaluations lay the foundation for improved well-being and better quality of life. In the next chapter, we'll explore the behavioral therapies that can help individuals address eating challenges, focusing on practical strategies for change and adaptation.

Chapter 15

Assessing Co-Occurring Conditions

Eating disorders in autistic individuals often exist alongside other co-occurring conditions, such as anxiety, obsessive-compulsive disorder (OCD), sensory processing disorders, or gastrointestinal issues. These conditions can amplify the challenges associated with eating and complicate intervention strategies. This chapter explores how to recognize, assess, and manage these co-occurring conditions to support a holistic approach to treatment.

15.1 Why Co-Occurring Conditions Matter

Co-occurring conditions significantly influence eating behaviors and outcomes in autistic individuals:
- **Interconnected Symptoms**: Anxiety or OCD can drive food-related fears, rituals, or avoidance.
- **Treatment Complexity**: Addressing eating challenges without managing co-occurring conditions may yield limited success.
- **Impact on Quality of Life**: Untreated co-occurring conditions can exacerbate stress, discomfort, and health risks.

15.2 Common Co-Occurring Conditions

1. Anxiety Disorders
- **Relevance**:
  - High prevalence in autistic individuals, often manifesting as general anxiety, social anxiety, or phobias.
  - Anxiety about food texture, appearance, or mealtime environments can lead to extreme food selectivity.
- **Signs to Watch For**:
  - Refusal to try new foods due to fear of the unknown.
  - Avoidance of eating in unfamiliar settings or with unfamiliar people.

- o Physical symptoms like nausea or stomach pain linked to food anxiety.

2. Obsessive-Compulsive Disorder (OCD)
- **Relevance**:
  - o OCD-related rituals or obsessions can impact eating habits.
  - o Examples include specific food preparation requirements or rigid eating sequences.
- **Signs to Watch For**:
  - o Insistence on eating only foods of a particular color or shape.
  - o Distress if meals are served differently from the usual routine.
  - o Rituals around cutting or arranging food before eating.

3. Sensory Processing Disorders
- **Relevance**:
  - o Sensory sensitivities to textures, smells, or flavors are common in autistic individuals.
  - o These sensitivities often overlap with or exacerbate eating challenges.
- **Signs to Watch For**:
  - o Refusal to eat foods with specific textures (e.g., crunchy or slimy).
  - o Overwhelming reactions to strong food smells or tastes.
  - o Preference for bland or monochromatic foods.

4. Attention Deficit Hyperactivity Disorder (ADHD)
- **Relevance**:
  - o Many autistic individuals also have ADHD, which can influence focus and regulation during mealtimes.
- **Signs to Watch For**:
  - o Difficulty staying seated or completing meals.
  - o Impulsive eating behaviors or overeating certain preferred foods.
  - o Disinterest in meals due to distractions or hyperfocus on non-food activities.

5. Gastrointestinal (GI) Disorders

- **Relevance**:
    - Common in autistic individuals, these disorders can contribute to discomfort and food aversions.
- **Signs to Watch For**:
    - Chronic constipation, diarrhea, or reflux.
    - Refusal of foods associated with past discomfort.
    - Difficulty digesting certain foods, such as those containing gluten or lactose.

15.3 Tools for Assessing Co-Occurring Conditions

1. Clinical Interviews

- Conducted with individuals and caregivers to explore behaviors, triggers, and symptoms related to both eating challenges and potential co-occurring conditions.

2. Questionnaires and Rating Scales

- **Examples**:
    - *Screen for Child Anxiety Related Disorders (SCARED)*: Evaluates anxiety symptoms.
    - *Yale-Brown Obsessive-Compulsive Scale (Y-BOCS)*: Measures OCD severity.
    - *Sensory Profile 2*: Assesses sensory sensitivities.

3. Behavioral Observations

- Professionals observe the individual in various settings, such as at home or during meals, to identify patterns and triggers related to eating and co-occurring conditions.

4. Collaboration with Specialists

- Gastroenterologists for GI issues.
- Psychiatrists for anxiety, OCD, or ADHD.
- Occupational therapists for sensory assessments.

15.4 Strategies for Managing Co-Occurring Conditions

1. Behavioral Therapies
- *Cognitive-Behavioral Therapy (CBT)*: Effective for anxiety and OCD, particularly when adapted for autistic individuals.
- *Exposure Therapy*: Gradual exposure to feared foods or situations in a controlled manner.
- *Applied Behavior Analysis (ABA)*: Focuses on positive reinforcement to encourage adaptive eating behaviors.

2. Medical Interventions
- Medications such as selective serotonin reuptake inhibitors (SSRIs) for managing anxiety or OCD.
- Dietary supplements or medications for treating GI conditions.

3. Environmental Modifications
- Creating predictable mealtime routines to reduce anxiety.
- Adjusting sensory elements, such as lighting or noise levels, to create a calming environment.

4. Education and Support for Caregivers
- Training caregivers to identify signs of co-occurring conditions and implement supportive strategies.
- Encouraging open communication about the individual's needs and preferences.

15.5 The Role of Multidisciplinary Teams
A collaborative approach ensures that all aspects of an individual's challenges are addressed:
- **Core Team Members**:
  - Pediatricians, psychiatrists, dietitians, occupational therapists, and psychologists.
- **Collaboration Goals**:
  - Share insights from different specialties to develop a comprehensive treatment plan.
  - Ensure consistent strategies across all areas of care.

15.6 Challenges in Managing Co-Occurring Conditions

- **Symptom Overlap**: It can be difficult to distinguish between symptoms caused by autism, eating disorders, or co-occurring conditions.
- **Resistance to Change**: Individuals may find it challenging to adapt to new routines or interventions.
- **Access to Resources**: Limited availability of specialized professionals in some areas can hinder comprehensive care.

15.7 Empowering Families

Empowering caregivers and families is key to successfully managing co-occurring conditions. Strategies include:
- **Building Knowledge**: Providing resources and education on common co-occurring conditions.
- **Encouraging Advocacy**: Supporting families in seeking appropriate care and interventions.
- **Offering Emotional Support**: Connecting families with support groups and counseling services.

15.8 Conclusion

Assessing and addressing co-occurring conditions is an essential part of understanding and managing eating challenges in autistic individuals. By recognizing the interplay between these conditions and eating behaviors, caregivers and professionals can create more effective, compassionate, and holistic care plans.

In the next chapter, we'll explore the behavioral and therapeutic approaches used to address specific eating challenges on the autism spectrum.

Chapter 16

Behavioral Therapy for ARFID and PICA

Behavioral therapy is one of the most effective approaches for managing Avoidant/Restrictive Food Intake Disorder (ARFID) and PICA, particularly when adapted to the unique needs of individuals with autism. This chapter explores various behavioral strategies, their application, and the adjustments required to make these therapies effective for those on the spectrum.

16.1 What is Behavioral Therapy?

Behavioral therapy focuses on identifying and changing behaviors that contribute to eating challenges. For ARFID and PICA, this involves:
- **Breaking Negative Associations**: Addressing fears, anxieties, or habits around eating.
- **Reinforcing Positive Behaviors**: Encouraging adaptive eating practices through rewards and motivation.
- **Gradual Desensitization**: Slowly introducing new foods or reducing harmful behaviors.

16.2 Behavioral Therapy for ARFID

For ARFID, therapy aims to increase food variety and reduce fear or avoidance behaviors.
1. Exposure Therapy
- **What It Does**:
    - Gradually introduces feared or avoided foods in a non-threatening way.
    - Helps reduce anxiety or sensory aversions associated with certain foods.
- **How It Works**:
    - Start with small, manageable goals (e.g., tolerating a disliked food on the plate without eating it).
    - Slowly progress to touching, smelling, or tasting the food.
    - Pair exposure with positive reinforcement to create positive associations.

2. Positive Reinforcement
- **What It Does**:
    - Encourages desired behaviors by rewarding progress, no matter how small.

- **Examples**:
    - Praising the individual for trying a new food.
    - Offering a favorite activity or token reward after successful exposure sessions.

3. Food Chaining
- **What It Does**:
    - Introduces new foods by leveraging existing preferences.
- **How It Works**:
    - Identify the individual's preferred foods (e.g., chicken nuggets).
    - Gradually introduce similar textures or flavors (e.g., baked chicken, chicken strips).
    - Expand the variety of foods over time while maintaining a sense of familiarity.

4. Modeling and Social Learning
- **What It Does**:
    - Encourages the individual to observe and imitate positive eating behaviors.
- **How It Works**:
    - Caregivers or peers model eating the targeted food calmly and enjoyably.
    - The individual is encouraged to join in a low-pressure setting.

16.3 Behavioral Therapy for PICA

For PICA, the primary goals are to reduce the consumption of non-food items and address the underlying triggers for this behavior.

1. Functional Behavior Analysis (FBA)
- **What It Does**:
    - Identifies the purpose or triggers of PICA behaviors, such as sensory-seeking or attention-seeking motives.
- **How It Works**:
    - Professionals observe the individual and document when and why PICA behaviors occur.

- o Develop interventions tailored to these triggers, such as providing alternative sensory input or addressing unmet needs.

2. Differential Reinforcement
- **What It Does**:
  - o Reinforces appropriate behaviors while discouraging harmful ones.
- **Examples**:
  - o Rewarding the individual for engaging with safe sensory alternatives, such as chewing gum or fidget toys.
  - o Ignoring or redirecting the behavior when non-food items are consumed (if safe).

3. Sensory Substitution
- **What It Does**:
  - o Provides safe alternatives to fulfill sensory needs.
- **How It Works**:
  - o Offer edible items with similar textures or sensory qualities to the non-food items being consumed.
  - o Examples: Replacing paper consumption with rice crackers or crunchy snacks.

4. Environmental Modifications
- **What It Does**:
  - o Reduces access to non-food items that might be ingested.
- **How It Works**:
  - o Remove hazardous items from the individual's immediate environment.
  - o Implement safety measures, such as locking cabinets or using visual cues to signal unsafe items.

16.4 Adaptations for Autistic Individuals

Behavioral therapies must be adapted to align with the unique needs and preferences of autistic individuals.

1. Emphasizing Predictability

- Use visual schedules or social stories to explain therapy sessions and set clear expectations.
- Maintain consistency in routines to reduce anxiety and foster trust in the process.

2. Incorporating Sensory Needs

- Adjust foods or environments to match sensory preferences.
- Include sensory breaks or calming strategies during therapy sessions.

3. Building Trust and Rapport

- Work at the individual's pace to avoid overwhelming them.
- Prioritize their comfort and autonomy in trying new foods or behaviors.

4. Collaborative Goal-Setting

- Involve the individual and caregivers in setting realistic, meaningful goals.
- Celebrate every achievement, no matter how small, to build confidence and motivation.

16.5 Involving Caregivers in Therapy

Caregivers play a vital role in the success of behavioral therapy:

- **Reinforcing Strategies at Home**: Consistently applying the techniques learned in therapy sessions.
- **Tracking Progress**: Documenting successes and challenges to inform therapy adjustments.
- **Providing Emotional Support**: Encouraging and reassuring the individual throughout the process.

16.6 Challenges in Behavioral Therapy

Behavioral therapy can be highly effective, but it's not without its challenges:

- **Resistance to Change**: Some individuals may struggle with adapting to new foods or behaviors.
- **Sensory Overload**: Therapy sessions may become overwhelming without careful pacing.

- **Need for Long-Term Commitment**: Progress is often gradual and requires sustained effort from all involved.

16.7 Case Studies and Success Stories

Highlighting real-life examples of individuals who benefited from behavioral therapy can provide inspiration and practical insights:
- A child with ARFID who expanded their diet from three foods to over a dozen through exposure therapy.
- An adolescent with PICA who replaced paper-eating with safe alternatives and reduced the behavior significantly.

16.8 Conclusion

Behavioral therapy offers powerful tools for managing ARFID and PICA, especially when tailored to the needs of autistic individuals. By addressing the behaviors and underlying triggers associated with these eating challenges, therapists, caregivers, and individuals can work together to build healthier, more adaptive eating habits.
The next chapter will delve into sensory integration techniques and their role in addressing sensory-based eating challenges.

Chapter 17

Sensory Integration Therapy

Sensory sensitivities play a significant role in the eating challenges faced by individuals on the autism spectrum. Sensory Integration Therapy (SIT) is a therapeutic approach designed to help individuals process sensory information more effectively, reducing discomfort and improving their ability to interact with their environment. This chapter explores how SIT can specifically address food-related sensitivities, fostering a healthier relationship with eating.

17.1 What is Sensory Integration Therapy?

Sensory Integration Therapy focuses on helping individuals regulate their responses to sensory input by exposing them to controlled sensory experiences. For individuals with autism, it aims to:
- Reduce overreaction or underreaction to sensory stimuli.
- Build tolerance to various textures, smells, and flavors of food.
- Improve overall sensory processing to decrease mealtime distress.

17.2 Sensory Sensitivities in Eating

Food-related sensory sensitivities can manifest in various ways:
- **Texture Sensitivity**: Avoiding foods that are slimy, crunchy, or grainy.
- **Taste Sensitivity**: Reacting strongly to bitter, spicy, or overly sweet flavors.
- **Smell Sensitivity**: Refusing foods with strong or unfamiliar odors.
- **Visual Sensitivity**: Preferring foods that look uniform or avoiding those with mixed colors and shapes.

These sensitivities can lead to restricted diets, heightened anxiety, and frustration during mealtimes.

17.3 How Sensory Integration Therapy Helps

1. Gradual Exposure to Sensory Input
- SIT introduces sensory stimuli in a controlled, non-threatening way.
- For eating, this might involve:

- o Touching food textures without eating.
- o Smelling foods to build familiarity.
- o Experimenting with small tastes of challenging foods over time.

2. Building Sensory Tolerance
- Therapy focuses on desensitizing individuals to specific sensory triggers.
- Example: A child sensitive to crunchy textures might gradually progress from touching a cracker to eventually eating one.

3. Enhancing Sensory-Motor Skills
- SIT activities strengthen the connection between sensory input and motor responses.
- Improved sensory-motor skills can help individuals manage food-related tasks like chewing and swallowing more effectively.

4. Creating Positive Sensory Experiences
- Encouraging interaction with food in playful, stress-free ways can reduce negative associations.
- Example: Playing games with foods of different colors or shapes before introducing them as edible options.

17.4 Techniques Used in Sensory Integration Therapy

1. Sensory Play
- Engages individuals in activities designed to explore different textures and sensations.
- Examples:
  - o Playing with non-food items like sand, slime, or water to build tolerance to tactile sensations.
  - o Using food-related items in sensory bins, such as dried pasta or rice.

2. Food Exploration Activities
- Encourages interaction with food outside of mealtimes.
- Examples:
  - o Allowing individuals to touch and smell foods without the pressure to eat.

- Involving them in food preparation, like peeling or mixing ingredients.

3. Oral Sensory Tools
- Helps individuals adjust to the feeling of different textures in their mouths.
- Examples:
  - Using vibrating toothbrushes to desensitize oral sensitivity.
  - Introducing safe chewable tools to mimic food textures.

4. Structured Sensory Diets
- A "sensory diet" is a personalized plan of sensory activities tailored to the individual's needs.
- For food sensitivities, this might include exposure to specific textures, smells, or tastes in a gradual and structured way.

17.5 Adaptations for Food-Related Sensitivities

1. Customizing the Approach
- Tailor therapy to the individual's specific sensory triggers.
- Example: If a child avoids slimy textures, start with slightly sticky textures and progress gradually.

2. Incorporating Preferred Sensory Input
- Use sensory stimuli the individual enjoys to create a positive experience.
- Example: Pairing a challenging food with a calming sensory activity, like listening to soothing music.

3. Respecting Sensory Limits
- Avoid overwhelming the individual by pushing too quickly.
- Observe and respond to cues indicating discomfort or overstimulation.

17.6 The Role of Caregivers in Sensory Integration Therapy

Caregivers play a vital role in reinforcing SIT strategies at home:
- **Encouraging Sensory Exploration**: Provide opportunities for sensory play and food exploration in a safe environment.
- **Modeling Positive Behavior**: Demonstrate enjoyment and openness to trying new foods.
- **Creating a Calm Mealtime Environment**: Reduce sensory overload by minimizing distractions and adjusting lighting, noise, or smells.

17.7 Success Stories

Highlighting real-life examples showcases the transformative potential of SIT:
- A young child who overcame a fear of slimy textures and began eating yogurt after weeks of sensory play.
- An adolescent who expanded their diet from beige foods to include fruits and vegetables through gradual exposure techniques.

17.8 Challenges and Limitations of SIT

While SIT offers promising results, challenges remain:
- **Time and Consistency**: Progress can be slow and requires sustained effort from therapists, caregivers, and individuals.
- **Sensory Overload Risks**: Poorly paced therapy can lead to increased anxiety or resistance.
- **Access to Services**: Availability of trained sensory integration therapists may be limited in some areas.

17.9 Conclusion

Sensory Integration Therapy provides a structured, supportive way to address sensory sensitivities related to food in individuals with autism. By gradually desensitizing individuals to sensory triggers and building positive associations with eating, SIT can foster healthier, more varied diets and reduce mealtime stress.

In the next chapter, we will examine the role of nutritional therapy in managing eating challenges and ensuring individuals on the spectrum receive balanced, adequate nutrition.

Chapter 18

Occupational Therapy and Eating Skills

Occupational therapy (OT) plays a crucial role in helping individuals on the autism spectrum improve their eating habits and mealtime behaviors. Many individuals with autism experience significant challenges with food, whether due to sensory sensitivities, motor difficulties, or behavioral issues. Occupational therapists work to enhance these individuals' abilities to engage in daily activities, including eating, by focusing on the skills necessary for successful mealtimes. This chapter explores how OT supports food acceptance and improves mealtime behaviors, ultimately fostering independence and better nutrition.

18.1 What is Occupational Therapy?

Occupational therapy is a therapeutic approach that helps individuals develop, recover, or maintain the skills necessary to perform everyday activities, or "occupations." For individuals with autism, this includes:

- **Sensory integration**: Addressing how sensory sensitivities affect daily functioning, including eating.
- **Fine motor skills**: Helping individuals improve coordination needed for tasks like feeding themselves.
- **Self-regulation**: Teaching strategies to manage emotions and behavior during mealtimes.

In the context of eating, occupational therapy focuses on improving food-related behaviors, addressing sensory issues, and promoting independence in mealtime tasks.

18.2 Key Areas Occupational Therapy Addresses in Eating

1. Sensory Sensitivities

- Many individuals with autism have heightened sensitivity to textures, tastes, and smells of food. Occupational therapists help by:
  - Gradually introducing different food textures to reduce aversions.
  - Using sensory strategies, like tactile play with food, to help desensitize sensory responses.
  - Employing techniques to encourage interaction with various food smells, colors, and presentations.

2. Motor Skills

- Feeding involves a range of motor skills, from holding utensils to chewing and swallowing. OT helps by:
    - Improving hand-eye coordination to facilitate self-feeding.
    - Strengthening fine motor skills for handling utensils and cups.
    - Working on oral motor skills to support chewing and swallowing, especially for individuals with oral sensitivities or motor difficulties.

3. Self-Feeding Independence

- For individuals who rely on caregivers to assist with feeding, OT works to promote self-feeding skills:
    - Encouraging the use of utensils and drinking from a cup.
    - Helping individuals develop the coordination needed to bring food to their mouths, chew, and swallow.
    - Providing strategies for promoting appropriate mealtime behaviors, like sitting at the table or following a mealtime routine.

4. Mealtime Routines and Behavioral Support

- Mealtimes can often be stressful, with sensory overload or behavioral challenges interfering with eating. OT can support by:
    - Developing a consistent mealtime routine to create structure and predictability.
    - Teaching calming techniques, like deep breathing or using fidget tools, to help regulate emotions during meals.
    - Reinforcing positive mealtime behaviors through reward systems and visual schedules.

18.3 Techniques Used in Occupational Therapy for Eating Skills

1. Sensory Desensitization
- Gradually exposing the individual to foods with challenging textures or smells in a non-threatening manner.
    - Start with food exposure outside of mealtime, such as touching or smelling food without eating it.
    - Gradually incorporate foods into meals once the individual is more comfortable interacting with them.
    - Offer a variety of textures in a controlled and predictable manner, such as crunchy or smooth foods, to build tolerance.

2. Oral Motor Exercises
- Oral motor therapy helps individuals develop the skills needed for chewing and swallowing.
    - Therapists may use specific tools like vibrating oral toys, chewy tubes, or straws to help individuals develop the muscles necessary for eating.
    - Exercises to strengthen the jaw and tongue muscles can make it easier to eat a wider range of foods.

3. Mealtime Structuring
- Creating a structured environment and routine around mealtimes is essential for reducing anxiety and promoting success.
    - Visual schedules or social stories can outline what will happen during a meal, helping individuals feel more prepared and in control.
    - Occupational therapists may encourage the use of timers to help individuals focus on the mealtime rather than becoming overwhelmed or distracted.

4. Behavioral Interventions

- OT often works with behavioral therapists to create strategies that encourage food acceptance and positive mealtime behaviors.
  - Reinforcement techniques: Rewarding small steps of progress, such as taking a bite of a new food or sitting at the table for a set amount of time.
  - Redirection: Using gentle cues to redirect inappropriate behaviors, such as food refusal or avoidance.

18.4 The Role of Caregivers in Occupational Therapy for Eating

Caregivers play a key role in supporting the goals of occupational therapy:

- **Implementing Strategies at Home**: Practicing mealtime routines, using visual aids, and applying sensory integration techniques.
- **Reinforcing Progress**: Recognizing small successes, such as trying new foods or using utensils independently, and celebrating them.
- **Collaborating with Therapists**: Sharing insights about the individual's preferences, triggers, and behaviors to adjust the therapy approach as needed.

18.5 Challenges in Occupational Therapy for Eating Skills

While OT can be highly effective, there are several challenges that may arise:

- **Resistance to New Foods**: Many individuals with autism have deep food preferences, and introducing new foods can be slow and difficult.
- **Sensory Overload**: Some individuals may become overstimulated during sensory exposure, making it harder for them to participate in therapy.
- **Consistency**: Achieving progress requires consistent practice, which can be difficult to maintain in a busy household.

18.6 Case Studies and Success Stories

Illustrating the positive outcomes of OT in real-life situations:
- A young child who transitioned from only eating five foods to accepting a more varied diet, using gradual sensory exposure and structured mealtimes.
- An adolescent with fine motor delays who learned to feed themselves independently through consistent practice and oral motor therapy.

18.7 Conclusion

Occupational therapy plays a vital role in improving food acceptance and mealtime behavior for individuals with autism. By addressing sensory sensitivities, improving fine motor skills, and creating a structured environment, OT helps individuals develop the skills necessary for healthy eating habits. Through a collaborative approach with caregivers and other professionals, individuals on the spectrum can achieve greater independence and better nutrition.

In the next chapter, we will explore the role of nutritional therapy in supporting individuals with eating challenges on the spectrum, ensuring their dietary needs are met while addressing food-related concerns.

Chapter 19

The Role of Nutrition Therapy

Nutrition therapy plays a pivotal role in addressing dietary deficiencies and guiding individuals on the autism spectrum toward a more balanced, nutritious diet. Many individuals with autism experience selective eating patterns, aversions to certain food groups, and difficulties with mealtime routines. These challenges can result in inadequate nutrition, potentially leading to long-term health issues. Nutrition therapy, when integrated with other therapeutic interventions, can help ensure individuals receive the essential nutrients needed for optimal growth, development, and overall well-being. This chapter explores the importance of nutrition therapy, its role in supporting dietary needs, and strategies used to promote a balanced diet.

19.1 What is Nutrition Therapy?

Nutrition therapy is a specialized area of care that focuses on using diet and nutrition to treat or prevent various health conditions. For individuals on the autism spectrum, nutrition therapy involves:

- **Assessing Nutritional Status**: Evaluating current eating habits and identifying nutritional gaps.
- **Personalized Diet Plans**: Creating individualized dietary recommendations that address specific needs, preferences, and sensitivities.
- **Managing Food Challenges**: Addressing issues such as food selectivity, gastrointestinal concerns, and other food-related difficulties.
- **Supporting Growth and Development**: Ensuring individuals meet age-appropriate nutritional milestones.

In the context of autism, nutrition therapy is particularly valuable in addressing common issues like food aversions, limited food choices, and the risk of nutrient deficiencies.

19.2 Common Nutritional Deficiencies in Autism

Individuals with autism often have highly selective eating habits, which can result in significant nutritional deficiencies. Common deficiencies include:

- **Vitamin D**: Essential for bone health and immune function, vitamin D deficiencies are common in individuals who avoid fortified foods or have limited outdoor exposure.
- **Calcium**: With a preference for limited food types like dairy, calcium deficiency can lead to bone weakness and other health issues.
- **Iron**: Low iron levels are often seen in individuals with restricted diets, leading to fatigue, weakness, and developmental delays.
- **Omega-3 Fatty Acids**: These are critical for brain function and emotional regulation, but many individuals with autism avoid fatty fish or other sources.
- **Fiber**: Due to a preference for processed or low-fiber foods, constipation and other gastrointestinal issues are common in autistic individuals.
- **B Vitamins**: Deficiencies in folate, B6, and B12 can affect mood, energy levels, and cognitive function.

Nutrition therapy can help identify these deficiencies and recommend strategies to correct them through dietary adjustments or supplements.

19.3 How Nutrition Therapy Works

Nutrition therapy for individuals with autism focuses on creating a balanced diet that addresses deficiencies, incorporates sensory preferences, and supports overall health. Some key components include:

1. Comprehensive Nutritional Assessment

- A detailed assessment of the individual's current eating habits, food preferences, and any existing medical concerns is the first step.
- The therapist may look for patterns of food selectivity, identify restricted food groups, and evaluate any gastrointestinal issues, such as constipation or food intolerances.

2. Developing a Tailored Nutrition Plan

- Based on the assessment, a nutrition plan is created to provide a balanced diet that meets the individual's specific needs.
- The plan takes into account:
    - Preferred foods and acceptable textures.
    - Sensory issues related to food (e.g., avoiding certain textures, tastes, or smells).
    - Health conditions (e.g., gluten sensitivity, lactose intolerance).
    - Special dietary needs (e.g., if supplementation is required).

3. Gradual Introduction of New Foods

- Nutrition therapists use strategies to introduce new foods slowly and in a non-threatening way. This can be done through:
    - **Food play**: Allowing the individual to interact with food outside of mealtime.
    - **Taste exploration**: Encouraging small tastes of new foods in a calm, non-pressuring environment.
    - **Food pairing**: Combining unfamiliar foods with preferred ones to increase acceptance.

4. Supplementation and Fortification

- For individuals who continue to have difficulty with food variety, supplementation may be necessary.
- Common supplements might include:
    - **Multivitamins**: To fill in nutrient gaps.
    - **Probiotics**: To address digestive concerns, such as constipation or irritable bowel syndrome (IBS).
    - **Fiber supplements**: If dietary fiber intake is insufficient.

5. Monitoring and Adjusting the Plan

- Nutrition therapy is an ongoing process that requires regular follow-up. The nutrition plan is adjusted based on the individual's response to changes, progress in food acceptance, and improvements in nutritional status.

- Regular check-ins help ensure that the individual's diet remains balanced and that new challenges are addressed as they arise.

19.4 Role of Nutrition Therapy in Behavioral Management

Nutrition therapy also plays a role in supporting behavioral outcomes. A balanced diet can improve mood, focus, and overall behavior. For example:
- **Blood sugar stability**: Avoiding sugar crashes through balanced meals can help with irritability and hyperactivity.
- **Omega-3s and brain function**: Including omega-3-rich foods can improve cognitive function, emotional regulation, and social interaction.
- **Gut-brain connection**: A healthy gut, supported by proper nutrition, can positively impact mood and behavior in individuals with autism.

Incorporating nutrition therapy into behavioral treatment plans can enhance the effectiveness of other interventions, such as behavioral therapy or occupational therapy.

19.5 Challenges in Nutrition Therapy

While nutrition therapy offers many benefits, there are also challenges that must be addressed:
- **Food aversions and selectivity**: Overcoming strong food preferences or aversions can be a slow and frustrating process.
- **Sensory sensitivities**: Individuals may refuse to eat certain foods due to texture, smell, or appearance, making it difficult to introduce a varied diet.
- **Lack of willingness to try new foods**: Many individuals with autism struggle with change, so introducing new foods may require patience and creativity.
- **Family and caregiver involvement**: Ensuring caregivers are committed to supporting the nutrition plan at home is essential for success.

19.6 Success Stories and Case Studies

Real-life examples help illustrate the impact of nutrition therapy:
- A teenager with selective eating habits began incorporating more fruits and vegetables into their diet after months of gradual exposure and support from a nutrition therapist.
- A young child who struggled with chronic constipation saw significant improvements after adding fiber-rich foods and probiotics to their diet, leading to better digestion and overall mood.

19.7 Conclusion

Nutrition therapy is a critical aspect of supporting individuals with autism to achieve a balanced, nutritious diet. By addressing sensory issues, promoting healthier food choices, and preventing nutritional deficiencies, nutrition therapists play a key role in improving both physical and mental health. In collaboration with other therapeutic approaches, nutrition therapy helps ensure that individuals on the spectrum can thrive, supporting their growth, development, and quality of life. The next chapter will explore how caregivers and educators can implement these strategies at home and in school settings to further enhance the effectiveness of nutrition therapy and mealtime management.

Chapter 20

Building Food Tolerance Gradually

For many individuals on the autism spectrum, introducing new foods into their diet or increasing diet diversity can be a slow and challenging process. This chapter focuses on strategies for gradually building food tolerance, helping individuals become more willing to explore a wider variety of foods in a safe and supportive way. By focusing on gradual exposure, consistency, and sensory-friendly approaches, individuals can expand their diet without feeling overwhelmed or anxious. This approach also helps to address sensory sensitivities, food preferences, and other barriers that may be contributing to limited food choices.

20.1 The Challenge of New Foods

For individuals with autism, food selectivity is a common challenge. Many struggle to try new foods due to sensory sensitivities, anxiety, or behavioral issues. The thought of changing their diet can be particularly overwhelming, leading to avoidance or rejection of new food options. Building food tolerance gradually is crucial for helping individuals expand their diet in a way that feels less intimidating and more manageable. This chapter provides practical strategies and tools for doing so.

20.2 Sensory-Friendly Strategies for Introducing New Foods

Sensory sensitivities often make food exploration difficult for individuals with autism. By making small adjustments and using sensory-friendly strategies, it's possible to increase acceptance and help build tolerance. Some strategies include:

1. Use Preferred Foods as a Bridge

- For many individuals, it's easier to introduce new foods if they're presented alongside something familiar. For example, combining new foods with a well-liked dip or sauce might make them more appealing. This gradual exposure method helps ease the transition and helps the individual explore different tastes, textures, and smells without feeling overwhelmed.

2. The "One-Bite Rule"

- This strategy involves encouraging an individual to try just one bite of a new food without any pressure to eat more. The goal is to expose the person to the food in a low-stakes, non-threatening way, which can help desensitize sensory responses over time. The one-bite rule can be used during snacks, meals, or even in food play sessions with other family members.

3. Minimize Sensory Overload

- Many individuals with autism struggle to focus or tolerate new foods due to sensory overload. To help, it's important to create a calm and predictable environment for eating. This might involve dimming the lights, using quiet music, or eliminating background noise during mealtime. Reducing distractions can help an individual focus more on the food itself, making it easier to explore new options.

20.3 Gradual Exposure Techniques

The gradual exposure technique involves exposing individuals to new foods in a systematic and controlled manner, with a focus on sensory comfort and acceptance. Here's how it works:

1. Start with Food Play

- Before introducing a new food at the dinner table, it can be helpful to explore it in non-meal situations first. This might involve touching, smelling, or playing with the food in a safe, relaxed environment. The goal is to help the person feel more comfortable and less threatened by the new food before it's actually introduced to their plate.

2. Present Foods in Different Forms

- Some individuals may be more willing to try a food if it's presented in a different way or with a familiar twist. For instance, a raw vegetable may be more palatable if it's cut into bite-sized pieces, mixed into a sauce, or grilled. By varying the form, flavor, or texture of the food, it becomes easier for the individual to accept new options over time.

3. Use Visual or Sensory Cues

- Visual supports, like photos, drawings, or charts, can be very helpful for introducing new foods to individuals who struggle with verbal communication or abstract concepts. Providing visual cues about what a new food looks like, how it might taste or smell, or where it fits in their food preferences can help reduce anxiety and increase acceptance.

20.4 Making Mealtime More Predictable and Comfortable

Predictability and routine are key for individuals with autism when it comes to trying new foods. By creating a structured and comfortable mealtime environment, it's possible to encourage greater food tolerance. Some tips for building predictability include:

1. Offer the New Food with Familiar Comfort Foods

- Providing a familiar comfort food alongside a new one is a great way to make the mealtime more predictable and less intimidating. For example, a serving of a favorite chicken nugget might be paired with a small taste of grilled chicken or steamed veggies. This helps build food tolerance over time without placing too much pressure on the individual.

2. Make the Environment Comfortable

- As previously mentioned, sensory-friendly strategies are important when introducing new foods. Make sure the environment is calm, with fewer distractions and a predictable atmosphere. Individuals with autism may benefit from using tools like fidget toys, chewies, or a weighted lap pad to help them focus during mealtime.

3. Keep It Simple

- Focus on introducing one new food at a time. Trying to introduce too many new items at once can be overwhelming for someone with autism. Break meals into smaller steps, such as one new vegetable at a time or one bite of a food during the meal, and gradually build up from there.

20.5 Rewards and Reinforcement

Rewards and reinforcement techniques can be highly effective when it comes to gradually increasing food tolerance. For example, giving praise, a small food reward (like a piece of their favorite fruit), or a token to use for future rewards can be highly motivating. This positive reinforcement system encourages individuals to try new foods, even if just a small bite, without overwhelming them with expectations.

20.6 Case Studies and Success Stories

Real-life examples help illustrate the effectiveness of gradual exposure techniques. For instance, a child who initially refused to eat more than five different foods was gradually able to expand their diet to include a wider variety of fruits, vegetables, and meats after using these techniques over a few months.

20.7 Conclusion

Building food tolerance gradually is essential for helping individuals with autism expand their diet without feeling anxious, overwhelmed, or pressured. By using sensory-friendly techniques, creating predictable mealtimes, and employing positive reinforcement, it's possible to support greater food acceptance and more balanced nutrition over time. With patience, persistence, and support from caregivers and nutrition therapists, individuals on the spectrum can continue to improve their eating habits and overall quality of life.

Chapter 21

Parental Training and Support

Parenting a child with autism can present unique challenges, especially when it comes to supporting positive eating behaviors and managing mealtime stress. This chapter focuses on how parents and caregivers can be equipped with the knowledge, tools, and strategies to help their child expand their food preferences, navigate eating challenges, and create a more enjoyable mealtime experience. Parental training and support are essential in reducing anxiety around food, fostering positive behaviors, and building healthy eating habits that will benefit both the child and the entire family.

21.1 The Role of Parents in Supporting Positive Eating Behaviors

Parents and caregivers are often at the forefront of supporting their child's eating habits. They play a crucial role in both the development of healthy eating behaviors and managing eating challenges. As the primary caregivers, parents can influence their child's food choices, the mealtime environment, and the types of interventions that are used to improve eating. Understanding the unique challenges their child faces is key to helping them navigate food selectivity, sensory sensitivities, and food-related anxiety.

Key roles parents play include:

- **Modeling Positive Eating Habits**: Children often imitate the behaviors of their caregivers. By demonstrating positive eating behaviors, such as trying new foods, maintaining a regular eating schedule, and showing a calm and open attitude toward food, parents can set an example for their children.
- **Creating a Structured Mealtime Routine**: Consistency is important for children with autism, and establishing regular meal times, along with predictable food choices, can reduce anxiety and stress around mealtime.
- **Reinforcing Positive Eating Behaviors**: Encouraging children with praise, rewards, or other forms of reinforcement when they try new foods or exhibit positive eating behaviors can create a more enjoyable and successful mealtime experience.

21.2 Understanding the Stress of Mealtime

Mealtime stress can be a common experience for both children with autism and their caregivers. This stress may come from a variety of sources, including:

- **Sensory Overload**: Children with autism may become overwhelmed by the textures, tastes, smells, or appearance of certain foods, leading to anxiety or refusal to eat.
- **Resistance to Change**: Children with autism often have rigid eating habits and may struggle with new foods or unfamiliar mealtime routines.
- **Parental Anxiety**: Parents can also feel stressed or anxious if their child is not eating properly or if mealtimes are fraught with conflict, which can further impact the child's food acceptance.
- **Social Pressure**: Parents may feel societal pressure to have their child eat "normally," which can heighten the stress of mealtimes and affect the child's comfort level around food.

Recognizing these sources of stress is the first step toward alleviating them. This chapter explores how parents can manage both their child's stress and their own to create a more positive eating environment.

21.3 Parental Training: Educating and Empowering Caregivers

One of the most effective ways to support parents and caregivers is through targeted training that helps them understand how to manage eating challenges and foster a positive relationship with food. Parental training should include education on:

1. Understanding Autism and Eating Challenges

- Parents need to understand how autism can affect eating behaviors. This includes the sensory sensitivities, food selectivity, and other factors that contribute to difficulties around food. Knowledge of these challenges empowers parents to approach mealtime with empathy and understanding rather than frustration.

- Parents should also be educated on the importance of nutrition, why some children are more prone to restrictive diets, and how to address these issues in a calm and structured way.

2. Positive Behavioral Strategies
- Training in **applied behavior analysis (ABA)** or other behavioral strategies can help parents learn how to reinforce positive eating behaviors. Parents can be taught how to use rewards and praise effectively to encourage their child to try new foods or eat within set mealtimes.
- **Positive reinforcement** should be emphasized over punitive approaches, focusing on reinforcing small successes, such as tasting a new food or eating a previously rejected item.

3. Sensory Strategies
- Given the sensory sensitivities that many children with autism experience, parents should learn how to use sensory strategies to create a less overwhelming mealtime environment. These might include introducing foods with different textures gradually, making food less "visually" or "tactilely" stimulating, or reducing sensory distractions in the environment during meals.
- Parents should also be taught how to identify their child's sensory triggers and how to work around them to make food more acceptable.

4. Managing Mealtime Routines
- Establishing a consistent mealtime routine can reduce stress and make mealtimes more predictable for children with autism. Parents should be trained on how to structure mealtimes to promote calmness and consistency.
- This might include regular meal times, sitting down to eat together as a family, and using visual schedules to show the sequence of events during meals (e.g., washing hands, sitting at the table, taking a bite of food).

- Providing time for exploration of new foods without pressure can also help the child become more comfortable.

5. Encouraging Flexibility
- For children with autism, flexibility is often a challenge. However, learning strategies to encourage flexibility around food and eating routines can be very helpful. Parental training should emphasize the importance of small steps toward flexibility, like gradually increasing the variety of foods offered or creating a calm, supportive atmosphere when food changes are introduced.
- Teaching children how to deal with food-related anxiety or frustration can help them become more open to food diversity.

21.4 Managing Parental Stress

Parental stress often arises when caregivers feel powerless or overwhelmed by their child's eating challenges. Therefore, training must include stress management techniques that help parents stay calm and confident in their caregiving. Strategies include:

1. Practicing Self-Care
- Parents must be encouraged to take time for themselves, whether it's through physical exercise, meditation, or simply finding moments of respite. Taking care of themselves is essential for maintaining their emotional well-being, which directly affects their ability to support their child.
- Regular self-care can reduce overall stress and improve a parent's ability to handle mealtime challenges.

2. Joining Support Groups
- Support groups, whether in-person or online, can provide valuable opportunities for parents to connect with others who are facing similar challenges. Sharing experiences, tips, and encouragement can reduce feelings of isolation and help parents feel more empowered.

3. Developing Realistic Expectations

- Parents should be reminded that progress with eating challenges is often slow and incremental. It's important to celebrate small victories and to be patient with setbacks. Training should focus on setting achievable, realistic goals to reduce frustration and increase motivation.

21.5 Accessing Professional Support

Lastly, parents should be made aware of the professional resources available to them. Nutritionists, speech therapists, occupational therapists, and behavioral therapists all play key roles in addressing eating difficulties in children with autism. Parental training should help caregivers understand how to work with these professionals and when to seek additional help for more specialized concerns.

21.6 Conclusion

Parental training and support are essential to creating a positive mealtime experience for both children with autism and their caregivers. By understanding the challenges of eating on the spectrum, implementing structured routines, using sensory-friendly strategies, and managing stress, parents can play an instrumental role in improving their child's relationship with food. With the right tools, training, and ongoing support, mealtime can become a more enjoyable and less stressful experience for everyone involved.

Chapter 22

Medical Interventions and Supplements

For some individuals with autism spectrum disorder (ASD), eating challenges may require more than just behavioral interventions or sensory strategies. In cases where restrictive eating patterns or nutritional deficiencies have a significant impact on health, medical interventions, including nutritional supplements and, in certain cases, medication, can play a vital role in managing symptoms and improving overall well-being. This chapter explores various medical interventions, the potential benefits of supplements, and the role of medications in treating eating disorders like ARFID and PICA in individuals with autism.

22.1 Nutritional Supplements: Addressing Deficiencies and Supporting Health

Children with autism are often at risk for nutritional deficiencies due to restrictive eating habits, including avoiding certain food groups or only eating a small range of familiar foods. These deficiencies can lead to a variety of health concerns, including stunted growth, weakened immune function, and poor cognitive development. Nutritional supplements can help fill in the gaps where a child's diet is lacking and support their overall health and development.

Commonly used nutritional supplements include:

1. Multivitamins

- Multivitamins are a broad-spectrum solution that can help provide a range of essential vitamins and minerals. Children with ASD who are selective eaters may not consume enough fruits, vegetables, or whole grains to meet all of their nutritional needs, and a multivitamin can ensure they get key nutrients like vitamin D, B12, and folate.
- It's important to consult with a healthcare professional to determine the appropriate dosage, as excess intake of certain vitamins can cause adverse effects.

2. Omega-3 Fatty Acids

- Omega-3 fatty acids, commonly found in fish oil supplements, are often recommended for children with autism due to their potential benefits for brain health and behavior. Some studies suggest that omega-3s may help reduce symptoms of hyperactivity, impulsivity, and irritability in children with ASD.
- Omega-3s also support cardiovascular health and may help reduce inflammation, which has been shown to play a role in some developmental disorders.

3. Vitamin D

- Vitamin D is critical for immune system health, bone development, and overall well-being. Many children with autism are found to have low levels of vitamin D, especially those with limited exposure to sunlight or a diet that lacks fortified foods.
- Supplementing vitamin D can help improve mood and sleep patterns, both of which may be disrupted in children with autism.

4. Probiotics

- Gut health is often a concern for children with ASD, as many experience gastrointestinal issues, such as constipation or diarrhea. Probiotics are beneficial bacteria that can help support a healthy gut microbiome and alleviate digestive issues.
- Some studies suggest that gut imbalances may contribute to behavioral symptoms of autism, and probiotics may improve both gastrointestinal and behavioral symptoms.

5. Zinc and Iron

- Deficiencies in minerals like zinc and iron are common in children with autism, especially those who avoid certain foods like meat and dairy products. Zinc is essential for immune function, and iron supports energy levels and cognitive function.
- Supplementing these minerals can help boost energy, improve focus, and address anemia, which may occur due to insufficient dietary intake.

22.2 Medication: When Is It Necessary?

While nutritional supplements can be helpful in addressing deficiencies and supporting general health, there are instances when medication may be necessary to manage specific eating disorders or co-occurring conditions in individuals with autism. In particular, medications may be used when ARFID or PICA significantly interfere with the person's ability to eat safely, grow properly, or maintain nutritional balance.

1. Medications for ARFID

- **Antidepressants (SSRIs)**: Selective serotonin reuptake inhibitors (SSRIs), often used to treat anxiety or depression, may help manage some of the psychological factors that contribute to ARFID, such as obsessive thoughts about food or fear of eating.
- **Appetite Stimulants**: Some medications, such as cyproheptadine, can help stimulate appetite in individuals with ARFID who have extremely limited food intake due to fear or sensory sensitivities. These medications can be used short-term to help encourage eating and support weight gain.
- **Cognitive Behavioral Therapy (CBT) with Medication**: In combination with therapy, SSRIs may help address the underlying anxiety or compulsive behavior that is often associated with ARFID. Cognitive behavioral therapy, which targets food-related anxieties and maladaptive eating habits, can be paired with medication to offer comprehensive treatment.

2. Medications for PICA

- **Antipsychotics**: In severe cases of PICA, particularly when the consumption of non-food items poses a danger to the individual's health, antipsychotic medications may be prescribed. These medications, such as risperidone or olanzapine, are often used to treat irritability and compulsive behaviors in individuals with autism.
- **Mood Stabilizers**: Medications like lithium may be used to help manage mood swings and impulsivity, which can contribute to PICA. These drugs can reduce the frequency of PICA episodes and help manage related behavioral concerns.

- **Behavioral Medication**: Sometimes medications that target impulsive or compulsive behaviors, such as selective serotonin reuptake inhibitors (SSRIs), may help manage PICA by reducing the underlying urges to eat non-food objects.

3. Co-occurring Conditions

- Many children with autism have co-occurring conditions such as anxiety, OCD, or ADHD, which can influence eating behavior. Medications for these conditions—such as stimulants for ADHD or anti-anxiety medications—may improve the child's ability to focus on mealtime and reduce anxiety-related food refusal.
- Treating these co-occurring conditions can, in turn, help improve eating behaviors and make interventions for ARFID or PICA more effective.

22.3 The Role of a Medical Professional

Given the complexities involved in diagnosing and managing eating challenges in individuals with autism, it is essential to work closely with a medical team. Healthcare providers, such as pediatricians, nutritionists, psychiatrists, and gastroenterologists, can help tailor medical interventions to meet the specific needs of the individual.

Medical professionals can:

- **Provide Individualized Treatment Plans**: Every child with autism has a unique combination of strengths and challenges. A healthcare professional can help create a personalized plan that addresses specific eating habits, food sensitivities, and nutritional deficiencies.
- **Monitor Progress**: Regular monitoring of the child's health and growth is essential to ensure that interventions are having the desired effects. This includes blood tests to check for deficiencies, as well as assessments of physical development.
- **Coordinate Care Across Disciplines**: Managing eating disorders in children with autism often requires input from multiple specialists, including dietitians, behavior analysts, and mental health professionals. Coordinating care ensures that all aspects of the child's health and behavior are addressed comprehensively.

22.4 Risks and Considerations of Medical Interventions

While medical interventions, including supplements and medication, can be helpful in managing eating challenges, they must be used carefully and under the guidance of a healthcare professional. Overuse or improper use of certain supplements can lead to toxicity, and medications often come with potential side effects, such as weight gain, sedation, or irritability. Therefore, parents and caregivers should:

- **Consult Regularly with Healthcare Providers**: Ongoing consultations ensure that medical interventions are appropriate, effective, and tailored to the individual's needs.
- **Monitor Side Effects**: Parents should be vigilant about any potential side effects that medications or supplements may cause, and report these to healthcare providers.
- **Integrate Medical Interventions with Other Approaches**: Medical treatments should be viewed as part of a comprehensive approach that includes behavioral interventions, dietary management, and other therapeutic strategies.

22.5 Conclusion

For individuals with autism who face eating challenges, medical interventions such as nutritional supplements and, in some cases, medications, can be crucial in supporting overall health and well-being. These interventions, when used in conjunction with other therapies and behavioral strategies, can help manage the symptoms of ARFID, PICA, and other eating difficulties on the spectrum. It is essential for parents and caregivers to work closely with healthcare professionals to ensure that medical treatments are safe, effective, and appropriately tailored to the unique needs of the child.

Chapter 23

Creating a Positive Mealtime Environment

Mealtime can be a source of stress for both individuals with autism spectrum disorder (ASD) and their caregivers, particularly when eating challenges such as ARFID, PICA, or food selectivity are present. Creating a positive mealtime environment can make a significant difference in helping individuals feel more comfortable and open to trying new foods, reducing anxiety around eating, and fostering healthier eating habits. This chapter explores strategies to cultivate a supportive, stress-free atmosphere at mealtimes, ensuring that food is viewed as a positive, nurturing experience rather than a source of conflict or anxiety.

23.1 The Importance of a Calm and Predictable Environment

For many individuals with autism, routine and predictability are essential to feeling secure and managing anxiety. The mealtime environment should reflect these needs, with a focus on minimizing distractions and maintaining consistency.

Key strategies include:

- **Consistent mealtimes**: Establish a regular eating schedule. Consistency helps to reduce anxiety and creates a sense of security, which is especially important for children with autism who thrive on routines.
- **Predictable meal settings**: Keep the meal setting consistent in terms of location, tableware, and seating arrangements. This can help individuals feel more at ease and focused on the meal rather than becoming distracted by changes in the environment.
- **Structured mealtime rituals**: Create a simple and consistent ritual for mealtimes, such as washing hands, setting the table together, or using a specific napkin. These rituals can signal to the individual that it's time to eat and help to set expectations for behavior during meals.

23.2 Minimizing Sensory Overload

Sensory sensitivities are common among individuals with autism, and these can make mealtimes overwhelming. Bright lights, loud noises, strong smells, and even the texture of food can cause discomfort and distress. Reducing sensory overload can help the person feel more relaxed and willing to engage with food.

Tips for minimizing sensory overload include:

- **Control sensory stimuli**: Limit distracting sounds, such as loud music or background TV, during meals. Dim the lights if necessary, as bright lighting can sometimes feel overwhelming.
- **Use familiar utensils and dishes**: Avoid overwhelming the person with unfamiliar items. Use dishes, cups, and utensils that the individual is comfortable with. Simple, plain plates may be more appealing than brightly colored ones that could feel visually distracting.
- **Be mindful of food textures and smells**: For individuals with sensory sensitivities, certain food textures or strong smells can be off-putting. Start by offering foods that are more neutral or less intense in terms of texture and scent, such as bland, soft foods, and gradually introduce new textures in a non-threatening way.

23.3 Encouraging Positive Food Experiences

Creating a positive association with food is crucial for helping individuals overcome food-related anxieties or aversions. By promoting enjoyment and curiosity around food, mealtime can become a more pleasant experience.

Key strategies to encourage positive food experiences include:

- **Make food visually appealing**: Present food in a visually pleasant and attractive manner. A well-arranged plate can spark curiosity and may make trying new foods seem more inviting.

- **Incorporate fun and playfulness**: For children, introducing food-related games or activities (such as "food art" where they can decorate their own plates) can make mealtime more enjoyable and reduce anxiety. These activities can encourage hands-on interaction with food in a low-pressure way.
- **Introduce new foods slowly**: Instead of overwhelming the person with a wide variety of new foods at once, introduce new items gradually, alongside familiar ones. This reduces pressure and makes trying new things feel less intimidating.
- **Focus on small portions**: Serve small portions to prevent overwhelming the individual with a large amount of food. This also gives them the chance to feel in control of the mealtime, which can reduce anxiety and encourage food acceptance.
- **Praise effort, not just eating**: Provide positive reinforcement for any attempts to try new foods or engage with mealtime, even if the person doesn't actually eat the food. Praising the effort shows that you value the process of exploring new foods, not just the outcome.

23.4 Reducing Mealtime Pressure

Mealtime pressure can cause anxiety, leading to refusal or avoidance of food. Creating an environment where the individual feels no pressure to eat can help alleviate anxiety and encourage them to engage with food at their own pace.
Strategies to reduce mealtime pressure include:
- **Avoid forcing or bribing**: Pushing someone to eat or offering rewards to eat a particular food can increase resistance and heighten food-related stress. Instead, gently encourage exploration without the expectation of eating everything on the plate.
- **Allow autonomy in food choices**: Whenever possible, give the individual some control over their food choices. For example, allow them to choose between two meal options, or let them pick out their own snacks. This promotes a sense of independence and can help reduce power struggles around food.

- **Offer choices, but don't overwhelm**: Offering too many options can be overwhelming. Present a few simple choices and let the individual decide. This reduces decision fatigue and increases the chances of the person choosing something they're comfortable with.
- **Keep the focus on mealtime, not eating**: Try to shift the focus of the mealtime away from just eating. Engage in relaxed conversation or focus on the social aspect of the meal to reduce the spotlight on the individual's eating behaviors.

23.5 Creating a Supportive Mealtime Routine for the Whole Family

Mealtime isn't just about the person with autism—it's an opportunity for the entire family to gather, bond, and share in a positive experience. Family members should model healthy attitudes toward food and eating, which can influence the individual's relationship with food.

Tips for creating a supportive mealtime routine for the family include:
- **Eat together as a family**: Having family meals can help foster a sense of togetherness and normality. It provides a positive example of eating behaviors and reduces feelings of isolation or frustration for the individual.
- **Encourage everyone to try new foods**: Modeling positive food behaviors by trying new foods or openly discussing the enjoyment of different flavors can make the individual feel less singled out. It's important for everyone to be involved in creating a supportive and relaxed mealtime environment.
- **Maintain calm and positive energy**: Keep the atmosphere calm, especially if the individual is having difficulty with eating. Use calm voices, avoid negative reinforcement, and ensure that mealtime feels like an enjoyable experience rather than a stressful or confrontational one.

23.6 Mealtime Adaptations for Sensory or Behavioral Challenges

Some individuals with autism may struggle with sitting at the table or engaging in mealtime routines due to sensory sensitivities or behavioral challenges. It's important to adapt the environment or mealtime expectations to suit their individual needs.

Adaptations include:

- **Use sensory-friendly seating**: Some individuals may prefer sitting in a specific spot, using a particular type of chair, or sitting on a comfortable cushion. Ensuring that seating is comfortable and familiar can help reduce anxiety.
- **Allow breaks during mealtime**: If the individual struggles to sit still for long periods, consider offering short breaks during mealtime, allowing them to return to the table once they feel ready. This can prevent feelings of frustration from building up.
- **Use visual schedules or cues**: For individuals who struggle with transitions or changes in routine, visual schedules or cue cards can help guide them through the mealtime process, from sitting at the table to finishing their meal.

23.7 Conclusion

Creating a positive mealtime environment is a critical component of managing eating challenges for individuals with autism. By focusing on routine, sensory comfort, reducing pressure, and fostering positive food experiences, caregivers and family members can help transform mealtimes into a more enjoyable and less stressful part of daily life. Patience, flexibility, and understanding are key, and with consistent effort, it's possible to encourage healthier eating habits, improve food acceptance, and create a positive relationship with food for individuals on the autism spectrum.

Chapter 24

Addressing Anxiety and Stress Around Food

For individuals with autism spectrum disorder (ASD), anxiety and stress around food are common barriers to healthy eating and nutrition. Anxiety may arise from sensory sensitivities, previous negative experiences with food, or a lack of control over mealtimes. This anxiety can exacerbate restrictive eating, making it more difficult to introduce new foods or overcome food aversions. Addressing anxiety and stress around food is crucial in helping individuals develop a more balanced relationship with food and mealtime routines. In this chapter, we explore various techniques and approaches that can help reduce food-related anxiety, making mealtimes more comfortable and less stressful.

24.1 Understanding the Root Causes of Anxiety Around Food

Before addressing anxiety, it's essential to understand its underlying causes. In individuals with ASD, food-related anxiety may stem from several sources, such as:

- **Sensory sensitivities**: Over-sensitivity to textures, smells, or tastes of food can trigger anxiety or discomfort, making certain foods unbearable.
- **Past negative experiences**: Previous experiences of choking, vomiting, or being forced to eat certain foods can create lasting associations of fear or distress.
- **Lack of control**: Some individuals may feel anxiety due to the lack of control over their food choices or mealtime environment. Having a predictable routine or being pressured to eat specific foods can exacerbate this stress.
- **Social pressures**: Meals in social settings, such as at school or during family gatherings, may introduce anxiety, especially when the individual feels different from others or is expected to behave in a typical manner.

By identifying the causes of food-related anxiety, caregivers can better tailor strategies to reduce stress and encourage a more relaxed approach to mealtime.

24.2 Creating a Calm and Predictable Mealtime Routine

As mentioned earlier, routine and predictability are vital for reducing anxiety in individuals with ASD. By creating a calm, structured, and familiar mealtime environment, anxiety can be significantly lowered, helping to ease stress and promote more positive food interactions.

Key strategies include:

- **Consistent meal times**: A consistent eating schedule provides stability and predictability, reducing the anxiety of uncertainty. Individuals with ASD often feel more comfortable when they know when they will be eating and what to expect.
- **Clear communication**: Use visual or verbal cues to signal the start of a meal. A visual schedule, countdown timer, or even verbal announcements such as "It's time for lunch" can help prepare the individual for the transition to mealtime, which can reduce anxiety.
- **Environmental predictability**: Ensure the mealtime setting is familiar. Consistency in seating, the table setting, and the people involved can help create a stable and less stressful environment.

24.3 Gradual Exposure to New Foods

The idea of trying new foods can be overwhelming for individuals with autism, especially those who already have restrictive eating habits due to anxiety. Gradual exposure to new foods, in a way that feels safe and non-threatening, can reduce food-related anxiety over time.

Techniques for gradual exposure include:

- **Start with familiar foods**: Introduce new foods alongside familiar ones. For example, place a new food on the plate next to a food the individual already likes. This reduces the pressure to engage with the new food while making its presence familiar.

- **Non-food related exposure**: Before attempting to eat a new food, engage the individual in non-food activities involving that food. For example, they can smell, touch, or even play with the food before tasting it. These less intense interactions can build comfort and familiarity.
- **Use "small steps"**: Break down the process of trying new foods into small, manageable steps. If the person is hesitant to try a new food, begin by having them look at it, then touch it, and finally, take a small bite. Praise each small step to reinforce progress and reduce anxiety.
- **Model positive behavior**: Eating the new food yourself can help normalize the experience and reduce anxiety. Be enthusiastic but non-pressuring about trying new foods, showing that it can be enjoyable and safe.

24.4 The Power of Positive Reinforcement

Reinforcing positive behavior related to food can help reduce anxiety and increase willingness to engage with food. Positive reinforcement can be used to acknowledge small victories and help foster an environment of encouragement rather than pressure.

Reinforcement strategies include:
- **Praise and rewards**: Celebrate attempts, no matter how small, to try new foods or engage with mealtime. Offer verbal praise, stickers, or tokens as rewards for progress, not necessarily for eating the food.
- **Focus on effort, not outcome**: Reinforce the process of engaging with food, rather than the actual consumption of it. For example, if the individual smells, touches, or tastes a new food, celebrate the effort regardless of whether they eat it.
- **Non-food rewards**: Use non-food rewards for meeting mealtime goals, such as extra playtime, a favorite activity, or a relaxing break. This ensures that food is not seen as the only source of reinforcement, reducing any unhealthy associations with eating.

24.5 Cognitive Behavioral Techniques to Manage Anxiety

Cognitive-behavioral therapy (CBT) can be an effective tool in reducing anxiety around food. CBT focuses on changing negative thought patterns and behaviors, helping individuals to reframe their experiences with food in a more positive light.

Techniques for addressing food-related anxiety through CBT include:

- **Cognitive restructuring**: Work with the individual to identify and challenge irrational fears or negative beliefs about food. For example, if a child believes that trying a new food will make them sick, help them recognize that this is unlikely and provide evidence to challenge that thought.
- **Relaxation techniques**: Teaching relaxation techniques, such as deep breathing, guided imagery, or progressive muscle relaxation, can help the individual manage stress and anxiety before or during mealtime.
- **Mindfulness**: Encourage mindfulness during meals. This practice can help the individual become more aware of their feelings, thoughts, and sensory experiences related to food, helping them to manage anxiety in real-time and focus on the present moment.

24.6 Reducing the Pressure to Eat

Pressure to eat can increase anxiety, especially for individuals with autism who may already have a limited food repertoire or heightened food-related stress. It's important to allow flexibility around eating, so that the individual does not feel coerced or stressed.

Key strategies for reducing pressure include:

- **Give control over food choices**: Allow the individual to make choices about what they eat. This gives them a sense of control and autonomy, which can reduce anxiety. For example, let them choose between a couple of meal options, or allow them to decide when to try new foods.

- **Non-food related exposure**: Before attempting to eat a new food, engage the individual in non-food activities involving that food. For example, they can smell, touch, or even play with the food before tasting it. These less intense interactions can build comfort and familiarity.
- **Use "small steps"**: Break down the process of trying new foods into small, manageable steps. If the person is hesitant to try a new food, begin by having them look at it, then touch it, and finally, take a small bite. Praise each small step to reinforce progress and reduce anxiety.
- **Model positive behavior**: Eating the new food yourself can help normalize the experience and reduce anxiety. Be enthusiastic but non-pressuring about trying new foods, showing that it can be enjoyable and safe.

24.4 The Power of Positive Reinforcement

Reinforcing positive behavior related to food can help reduce anxiety and increase willingness to engage with food. Positive reinforcement can be used to acknowledge small victories and help foster an environment of encouragement rather than pressure.

Reinforcement strategies include:
- **Praise and rewards**: Celebrate attempts, no matter how small, to try new foods or engage with mealtime. Offer verbal praise, stickers, or tokens as rewards for progress, not necessarily for eating the food.
- **Focus on effort, not outcome**: Reinforce the process of engaging with food, rather than the actual consumption of it. For example, if the individual smells, touches, or tastes a new food, celebrate the effort regardless of whether they eat it.
- **Non-food rewards**: Use non-food rewards for meeting mealtime goals, such as extra playtime, a favorite activity, or a relaxing break. This ensures that food is not seen as the only source of reinforcement, reducing any unhealthy associations with eating.

24.5 Cognitive Behavioral Techniques to Manage Anxiety

Cognitive-behavioral therapy (CBT) can be an effective tool in reducing anxiety around food. CBT focuses on changing negative thought patterns and behaviors, helping individuals to reframe their experiences with food in a more positive light.

Techniques for addressing food-related anxiety through CBT include:
- **Cognitive restructuring**: Work with the individual to identify and challenge irrational fears or negative beliefs about food. For example, if a child believes that trying a new food will make them sick, help them recognize that this is unlikely and provide evidence to challenge that thought.
- **Relaxation techniques**: Teaching relaxation techniques, such as deep breathing, guided imagery, or progressive muscle relaxation, can help the individual manage stress and anxiety before or during mealtime.
- **Mindfulness**: Encourage mindfulness during meals. This practice can help the individual become more aware of their feelings, thoughts, and sensory experiences related to food, helping them to manage anxiety in real-time and focus on the present moment.

24.6 Reducing the Pressure to Eat

Pressure to eat can increase anxiety, especially for individuals with autism who may already have a limited food repertoire or heightened food-related stress. It's important to allow flexibility around eating, so that the individual does not feel coerced or stressed.

Key strategies for reducing pressure include:
- **Give control over food choices**: Allow the individual to make choices about what they eat. This gives them a sense of control and autonomy, which can reduce anxiety. For example, let them choose between a couple of meal options, or allow them to decide when to try new foods.

- **Respect hunger cues**: Encourage eating when the individual is hungry, rather than forcing meals at specific times. If they are not hungry, respect their need to skip a meal or have a smaller portion.
- **Avoid using food as a reward or punishment**: This can create unhealthy associations with food. Instead, focus on offering food in a neutral and non-pressuring way.

24.7 Creating a Safe and Supportive Mealtime Environment

Finally, a safe, non-threatening mealtime environment is essential for reducing anxiety around food. This involves both physical and emotional support.

Creating a supportive environment involves:
- **Staying calm and patient**: Caregivers and family members should model calm behavior, as anxiety is often contagious. If the individual senses that others are stressed or frustrated, it can escalate their own anxiety.
- **Minimizing distractions**: Keep the focus on the meal by reducing distractions such as loud noise or television. This helps the individual stay centered on eating, rather than becoming overwhelmed by external stimuli.
- **Offering emotional support**: Validate the individual's feelings and provide reassurance. Acknowledge that mealtime can be difficult, but emphasize that it's okay to take small steps and make progress at their own pace.

24.8 Conclusion

Addressing anxiety and stress around food is a critical step in helping individuals with autism develop a healthier relationship with eating. By using strategies such as gradual exposure, positive reinforcement, and relaxation techniques, caregivers can help reduce food-related anxiety and create a more positive mealtime experience. Through patience, consistency, and understanding, it is possible to reduce stress around food, encourage a more varied diet, and create a sense of security and comfort during meals.

Chapter 25

Community and Support Networks

Navigating the challenges of eating disorders and food-related difficulties in individuals with autism can be overwhelming for families and caregivers. Finding resources and connecting with others who share similar experiences can provide crucial support and guidance. Community networks, including support groups, advocacy organizations, and professional resources, offer emotional encouragement, practical strategies, and shared knowledge. In this chapter, we explore the importance of building a robust support system for individuals with eating challenges and their families, and how engaging with the right community resources can make a significant difference in managing and overcoming these obstacles.

25.1 The Power of Peer Support

Peer support is one of the most valuable aspects of connecting with a community of individuals facing similar challenges. Whether through local support groups, online forums, or social media groups, peer support offers a sense of belonging and understanding that can help reduce feelings of isolation. For families and caregivers, it's comforting to know they are not alone in their journey and that others have faced the same struggles.

Benefits of peer support include:
- **Shared experiences**: Connecting with others who are going through similar situations can provide comfort and reassurance. Families can learn from one another's strategies, successes, and setbacks, which helps normalize their experiences.
- **Emotional support**: Peer support groups provide a safe space where individuals and families can express their feelings, fears, and frustrations without judgment. This emotional validation can reduce stress and provide a sense of solidarity.
- **Practical advice**: Other parents or caregivers who have dealt with similar eating challenges can offer practical solutions and creative ideas for managing food selectivity, addressing sensory sensitivities, or creating positive mealtime routines.

Peer support can be found through local organizations, online groups, and specialized forums dedicated to autism and eating disorders, including ARFID and PICA. These networks also provide opportunities to attend meetups, share resources, and form lasting connections.

25.2 Connecting with Autism and Eating Disorder Advocacy Organizations

Several national and local organizations are dedicated to supporting families facing the complexities of autism and eating disorders. These organizations often offer educational resources, professional guidance, and specialized programs that can help individuals with ASD and eating challenges navigate their journey.

Some well-known organizations include:
- **The Autism Society**: Provides a wide range of resources, including information on sensory issues, eating challenges, and strategies for managing ARFID and PICA in individuals with ASD.
- **The National Eating Disorders Association (NEDA)**: Offers resources and support for eating disorders, including information on ARFID and PICA. NEDA also has helplines and online resources for caregivers seeking advice.
- **FEAST (Families Empowered and Supporting Treatment of Eating Disorders)**: This organization focuses on supporting families of individuals struggling with eating disorders, offering workshops, webinars, and community-building opportunities.
- **ARFID Network**: A specialized organization that focuses on Avoidant/Restrictive Food Intake Disorder (ARFID), offering resources and tools for families and professionals alike.

Engaging with these organizations can provide families with access to expert advice, tailored resources, and direct support. Many of these groups also offer online or in-person events, webinars, and conferences where families can connect with others, learn new skills, and stay informed about the latest research and treatment options.

25.3 Online Communities and Social Media Groups

Online communities and social media platforms provide valuable support and educational opportunities for families and caregivers. These platforms allow individuals to connect with others from around the world, offering a wealth of shared knowledge and personal experiences. Social media groups, discussion boards, and online forums are excellent spaces for ongoing support, especially for families who may not have access to in-person groups due to geographical location or other barriers.

Benefits of online communities include:
- **Accessibility**: Online groups and forums can be accessed from anywhere, making them a convenient option for families who may not have local support groups. This is particularly helpful for those in rural or underserved areas.
- **24/7 availability**: Online communities offer the flexibility of participating at any time, whether it's for emotional support, sharing ideas, or seeking advice.
- **Diverse perspectives**: Connecting with individuals from various backgrounds and experiences can offer new insights, strategies, and coping mechanisms. This diversity fosters creativity in problem-solving and can help families feel less isolated.
- **Resource sharing**: Online communities are often filled with caregivers and professionals who share articles, research, book recommendations, and helpful links that can support families as they navigate eating disorders and autism.
-

Popular online platforms where support groups for autism and eating challenges exist include Facebook, Reddit, and specialized online forums. It's important for families to research and join groups that are moderated by professionals or experienced individuals to ensure that the information shared is accurate and supportive.

25.4 Professional Guidance and Support Networks

In addition to peer and community support, professional guidance plays a crucial role in managing eating challenges in individuals with autism. Access to healthcare professionals who specialize in eating disorders, autism, or both, can make a significant impact on an individual's progress.

Key professionals who can be part of a support network include:
- **Dietitians and nutritionists**: These professionals can offer tailored advice on managing restrictive diets, ensuring nutritional needs are met, and helping individuals expand their food repertoire in a safe and gradual manner.
- **Occupational therapists**: Occupational therapists help individuals manage sensory sensitivities related to food and develop strategies to tolerate different textures, smells, and tastes. They also help with mealtime routines and behavioral modifications.
- **Psychologists and behavioral therapists**: These professionals can provide cognitive-behavioral therapy (CBT) or other therapeutic approaches to help manage anxiety, stress, and food-related fears. Behavioral therapists may also help with reinforcing positive eating behaviors and breaking down restrictive food habits.
- **Pediatricians and primary care doctors**: Having a primary care doctor who is familiar with autism spectrum disorder and eating challenges is essential for regular health checkups, monitoring growth, and addressing any underlying medical issues related to food intake.

By building a network of professionals, families can ensure that they receive well-rounded support that addresses both the behavioral and physical aspects of eating challenges in ASD.

25.5 The Role of School and Social Services

School systems and social services can also be vital support networks for families facing eating challenges. Many schools have special education programs and staff trained to help students with autism manage food-related difficulties in a safe and supportive environment.

Key areas where schools and social services can assist include:
- **Individualized Education Plans (IEPs)**: For children with autism, an IEP can include strategies to support eating habits, mealtime routines, and food tolerance. This can involve creating a comfortable and accommodating environment for students during mealtimes.
- **Behavioral support staff**: Schools often have behavior specialists or counselors who can work with students to address food-related anxiety, encourage healthier eating habits, and provide support during meal transitions.
- **Social services**: Local social service agencies may offer resources or programs to help families access food assistance, meal planning, and support for managing eating disorders.

Involving these resources in the care plan can provide families with additional support and alleviate some of the burdens associated with managing eating challenges.

25.6 Building a Personal Support Network

While community resources are invaluable, it's also essential for families to build a personal support network. This network can include friends, extended family, and other trusted individuals who can provide emotional support and practical help.

Suggestions for building a personal support network include:
- **Educating family and friends**: Providing information about autism, ARFID, PICA, and eating challenges can help family members and friends better understand the situation and offer more effective support.

- **Requesting help**: Don't be afraid to ask for support, whether it's for meal prep, accompanying the individual to appointments, or simply offering a listening ear.
- **Fostering a circle of care**: A support network doesn't have to be large—having just a few key people who understand the challenges and can offer help or a break is invaluable.

25.7 Conclusion

Community and support networks are essential for families facing eating challenges related to autism spectrum disorder. Whether through peer support groups, professional resources, or building a personal support network, these connections provide emotional reassurance, practical guidance, and valuable information. By tapping into these resources, families can not only help manage the immediate challenges of eating disorders like ARFID and PICA but also create a lasting foundation of support for ongoing progress and well-being.

Chapter 26

Life Skills for Independence with Food

Developing independence with food is a key aspect of enhancing quality of life for individuals on the autism spectrum. While eating challenges such as ARFID (Avoidant/Restrictive Food Intake Disorder) and PICA are common, fostering a sense of autonomy around food can significantly improve both physical health and emotional well-being. Life skills that focus on building comfort with food, navigating mealtimes, and making independent choices are crucial for long-term success. This chapter explores practical strategies and skills that can help individuals on the spectrum gain greater control over their eating habits and feel empowered in their relationship with food.

26.1 Building Basic Mealtime Skills

Mealtime independence starts with learning the essential skills that help individuals navigate the process of eating in a self-sufficient manner. These skills vary based on an individual's developmental level but are foundational for establishing a sense of control and routine.

Key skills to focus on include:

- **Self-feeding**: Teaching how to use utensils, drink from a cup, and serve food appropriately. For some individuals, this may include working with an occupational therapist to improve fine motor skills for handling utensils.
- **Meal Preparation**: Depending on the person's age and ability, simple meal preparation tasks can foster confidence. This could involve tasks such as stirring ingredients, assembling sandwiches, or setting the table.
- **Hygiene and Cleanliness**: Teaching the importance of hygiene, including washing hands before meals and cleaning up after eating. These skills are vital for maintaining proper health and hygiene.

A structured, step-by-step approach helps break down complex tasks into manageable actions, making it easier for the individual to learn and practice these skills.

26.2 Gradual Exposure to New Foods

One of the most significant barriers to food independence for individuals on the spectrum is food selectivity. Gradual exposure to new foods can help reduce anxiety and increase the comfort level with a variety of foods.

Strategies to introduce new foods include:

- **Desensitization**: Slowly introducing foods with similar textures or colors to the familiar foods that the individual already accepts. This allows for a more gradual expansion of food choices without overwhelming them.
- **Food Chaining**: Starting with a food that is similar to a preferred item and gradually moving to new types of foods. For example, if the individual likes plain pasta, introducing pasta with mild cheese or a simple sauce can help transition toward a broader variety of foods.
- **Positive Reinforcement**: Encouraging the individual to try new foods with positive reinforcement, such as verbal praise, rewards, or a preferred activity once the goal is achieved. This makes trying new foods feel rewarding and less stressful.

It is important to be patient and allow the individual to take ownership of their food exploration. The process may take time, but small successes can lead to a greater variety of foods being accepted.

26.3 Navigating Sensory Sensitivities

Many individuals with autism have heightened sensory sensitivities, which can impact their ability to tolerate certain textures, tastes, or smells of food. Addressing these sensitivities through individualized strategies can help the person feel more comfortable with eating.

Approaches to sensory integration with food include:

- **Texture Sensitivity**: Start with food that has textures the individual finds tolerable and gradually introduce new textures in a controlled way. For example, if the person prefers crunchy foods, offering a soft food with a crunch (like a crunchy topping) can be a good introduction.

- **Taste Sensitivity**: Gradually blend familiar tastes with milder versions of new flavors. If strong tastes (like spicy or sour) are a problem, introduce them in very small quantities or pair them with more neutral flavors to ease the transition.
- **Smell Sensitivity**: If a person is sensitive to smells, it may be helpful to prepare food with fewer strong odors or serve it at room temperature rather than hot, which can intensify smells. Allowing them to become familiar with the sight and feel of food before approaching it with smell can reduce anxiety.

By integrating sensory preferences into mealtime routines, individuals with autism can feel more comfortable around food, increasing the likelihood of expanding their food options and building independence.

26.4 Building Food Planning and Choice-Making Skills

Another important aspect of food independence is developing the ability to plan and make choices around food. This can involve selecting meals, participating in grocery shopping, and making simple food decisions.

Key strategies for promoting food planning include:
- **Choice Boards or Visual Aids**: For individuals who have difficulty processing verbal information, using a choice board with pictures or a list of foods can help them express their preferences and make meal decisions independently.
- **Grocery Shopping Involvement**: Taking the individual to the grocery store to help pick out familiar foods or choose between options can help them build confidence in making food choices. This also gives them an opportunity to practice decision-making and social skills in a real-world context.
- **Meal Planning with Guidance**: Teaching how to plan meals with simple guidance can involve asking the individual to choose between two options for breakfast, lunch, or dinner. As they become more comfortable, they can gradually take on more responsibility for planning meals themselves.

Providing the individual with opportunities to make their own food decisions fosters autonomy and helps them take ownership of their eating habits.

26.5 Social Skills Around Food

For many individuals with autism, mealtime can be a social challenge. Understanding the dynamics of eating in social settings, such as at family dinners, in public, or at school, is an important skill to develop.

Strategies to improve social skills around food include:
- **Modeling Appropriate Behavior**: Demonstrating mealtime etiquette and social norms, such as using polite conversation, sharing food, or waiting for others to finish eating, can help individuals understand how to engage in social situations.
- **Role-Playing**: Using role-play to practice social scenarios related to food can be helpful. For example, practicing what to say if someone offers food or how to ask for a preferred food item can make social interactions at mealtimes easier.
- **Social Stories**: Writing or reading social stories about mealtime interactions, such as eating in a restaurant, can help individuals prepare for specific situations they may encounter.

By improving social skills related to food, individuals can enjoy more positive and less stressful mealtimes with family and peers, building greater independence in social and eating situations.

26.6 Encouraging Self-Advocacy in Food Choices

Encouraging self-advocacy around food involves teaching individuals with autism to express their needs, preferences, and concerns regarding food in a clear and respectful manner. This can involve speaking up about sensory sensitivities, food allergies, or food choices, ensuring their preferences are respected in a variety of settings.

Ways to encourage self-advocacy include:
- **Assertiveness Training**: Teaching the individual to use clear, direct language to express their food preferences or issues. This could include practicing how to politely say, "I don't like this food" or "This food is too spicy for me."
- **Developing Communication Skills**: For individuals with limited verbal communication, using augmentative and alternative communication (AAC) devices or picture communication systems can help them convey their food needs more effectively.
- **Promoting Independence in Food Choices**: In settings such as school or at social events, individuals should be encouraged to ask for what they want and make their own food decisions within a structured and supportive environment.

Self-advocacy is a powerful tool that empowers individuals on the spectrum to take charge of their food experiences, promoting a greater sense of autonomy and confidence.

26.7 Conclusion

Building life skills around food is a critical step in helping individuals with autism gain independence and comfort in their eating habits. By focusing on basic mealtime skills, gradual exposure to new foods, sensory integration, food planning, social skills, and self-advocacy, individuals can develop a healthier, more positive relationship with food. These skills not only improve dietary diversity but also foster greater confidence, autonomy, and overall well-being. Supporting individuals in becoming independent with food requires patience, creativity, and the right tools, but the rewards are invaluable in promoting a more fulfilling, self-sufficient life.

Chapter 27

Educational Resources and Advocacy

Education, advocacy, and awareness play a pivotal role in supporting individuals with eating disorders on the autism spectrum. These elements are crucial not only for improving understanding of the unique eating challenges faced by people with ASD but also for creating environments that are better equipped to support their needs. This chapter explores the importance of educational resources, the role of advocacy, and how greater awareness can positively impact both individuals and the communities that support them.

27.1 The Need for Education on ASD and Eating Disorders

Education is the cornerstone of any effective intervention or support system for individuals with eating disorders on the autism spectrum. Unfortunately, autism and its associated eating challenges are often misunderstood or overlooked, leading to delays in diagnosis, ineffective treatments, or unnecessary stigma.

Key educational goals include:

- **Raising Awareness of ASD-Related Eating Challenges**: Many professionals, educators, and even caregivers may not fully understand how eating disorders like ARFID or PICA manifest in individuals with autism. It's essential to educate them on the unique ways sensory issues, rigid thinking, and social communication challenges impact eating habits. This awareness can guide more effective interventions and promote greater empathy.

- **Training for Healthcare Providers**: Medical professionals, including pediatricians, dietitians, and therapists, must be equipped with specialized knowledge about how autism intersects with eating disorders. This training should focus on identifying early warning signs, providing accurate diagnoses, and offering tailored treatment plans.

- **Creating Supportive Environments**: Schools, daycares, and other institutions should be educated on how to support students with autism in managing their eating habits. Creating a positive and accommodating environment that recognizes sensory sensitivities, food selectivity, and the importance of routine can significantly improve outcomes.

Educational efforts should be designed to increase understanding at all levels of care and support, from the family home to the broader community, ensuring that individuals with autism receive the most appropriate care and attention.

27.2 The Role of Advocacy in Improving Support

Advocacy plays an essential role in improving access to resources, treatments, and accommodations for individuals with eating disorders on the autism spectrum. It involves raising awareness, influencing policies, and ensuring that the rights of individuals with autism are upheld, especially when it comes to their dietary needs and health.

Advocacy goals for supporting individuals with eating disorders include:

- **Advocating for Early Intervention**: One of the most important roles of advocacy is promoting early diagnosis and intervention. By recognizing the signs of eating disorders such as ARFID or PICA early, appropriate treatment can be provided, preventing long-term physical and psychological effects.
- **Promoting Tailored Treatment**: Eating disorder treatment plans for individuals with autism must be adapted to address sensory sensitivities, behavioral patterns, and communication needs. Advocates can help ensure that treatment providers offer autism-friendly approaches that consider these factors.

- **Legislation and Policy Changes**: Advocacy can also play a crucial role in pushing for legislative changes that address the specific needs of people with autism. This could include advocating for insurance coverage of specialized treatments for eating disorders, increased funding for autism research, or policies that require schools to provide accommodations for students with ASD-related eating challenges.

Advocacy is about amplifying the voices of individuals with autism and their families, making sure that their needs are understood, respected, and addressed in both healthcare and educational systems.

27.3 Increasing Public Awareness and Reducing Stigma

Public awareness and understanding of autism-related eating disorders can significantly reduce stigma and misconceptions. By educating the general public about the connection between autism and eating challenges, we can foster a more accepting and supportive environment for those affected.

Ways to increase awareness include:

- **Public Campaigns**: National and local awareness campaigns can help shed light on the unique challenges faced by individuals with autism regarding eating habits. These campaigns can highlight common issues such as food selectivity, sensory sensitivities, and compulsive eating behaviors, while also offering information on where families can seek support.
- **Community Education Programs**: Community-based education programs are essential in spreading knowledge about how eating disorders manifest in individuals with ASD. Workshops, seminars, and informational sessions can be offered to schools, healthcare providers, and community organizations to foster greater understanding and empathy.

- **Collaborations with Autism Organizations**: Working with organizations that advocate for autism can help amplify the message about eating disorders in the autism community. These partnerships can create a unified voice for the needs of individuals with ASD, ensuring that their challenges are recognized and addressed at every level.

Raising public awareness and reducing stigma helps ensure that individuals with autism are not isolated or misunderstood. It also enables families and caregivers to feel supported in their efforts to manage eating challenges.

27.4 Access to Specialized Resources

Access to the right resources is critical for families and individuals dealing with eating disorders on the autism spectrum. These resources provide the knowledge, tools, and support necessary to effectively manage eating challenges and improve overall well-being.

Specialized resources may include:

- **Autism-Specific Eating Disorder Clinics**: Clinics specializing in the treatment of autism-related eating disorders can offer tailored therapies that consider both the medical and behavioral aspects of the disorder. These clinics often have interdisciplinary teams, including psychologists, nutritionists, occupational therapists, and dietitians, who work together to create comprehensive treatment plans.
- **Support Groups for Families**: Support groups provide a vital space for parents and caregivers to share their experiences, gain advice, and learn about strategies that have worked for others. These groups also help reduce feelings of isolation and provide emotional support during challenging times.
- **Educational Materials and Books**: Books, articles, and online resources can offer valuable guidance on navigating the complexities of eating disorders in individuals with autism. These materials often provide practical tips, real-life stories, and evidence-based approaches that can help families manage eating challenges more effectively.

Ensuring that families have access to specialized resources empowers them to take an active role in supporting their loved ones and managing eating-related difficulties.

27.5 The Importance of Collaboration Between Professionals

Collaboration between professionals across different fields is essential for providing comprehensive care for individuals with autism and eating disorders. When healthcare providers, educators, and therapists work together, they can create a more holistic approach to treatment and support.

Key points for successful collaboration include:

- **Multidisciplinary Teams**: The best outcomes for individuals with eating disorders often arise from a team approach, where professionals from various disciplines—such as pediatricians, psychologists, dietitians, and occupational therapists—work together to create an individualized care plan.
- **Coordinated Care Across Settings**: Whether at home, school, or in healthcare facilities, coordinated care ensures that the strategies and interventions being used are consistent and support the individual's needs across all environments. This approach is especially important for individuals with autism, who may experience difficulties with transitions between different settings.
- **Shared Knowledge and Expertise**: By sharing knowledge, professionals can gain a better understanding of how autism intersects with eating challenges. This helps inform more effective treatment plans and encourages the development of autism-friendly approaches to addressing eating disorders.

Collaboration between professionals is a powerful way to ensure that individuals with autism receive comprehensive, effective support for their eating challenges.

27.6 Conclusion

Educational resources, advocacy, and public awareness are critical in supporting individuals with eating disorders on the autism spectrum. By promoting a deeper understanding of how autism affects eating habits, advocating for specialized care, and increasing access to resources, we can improve the quality of life for individuals with ASD. The collaboration between families, professionals, and the broader community helps create a supportive environment where individuals can thrive, build independence, and overcome eating challenges. Through education and advocacy, we can ensure that no one with autism faces eating disorders in isolation and that they receive the care, understanding, and support they need to succeed.

Chapter 28

Success Stories and Case Studies

In this chapter, we will highlight real-life success stories and case studies that demonstrate how individuals with autism and eating challenges, such as ARFID or PICA, have made significant progress. These stories showcase the power of early intervention, tailored treatment plans, and the support of dedicated professionals, caregivers, and families. By exploring these case studies, readers can gain hope and inspiration, learning how challenges can be overcome with the right strategies and perseverance.

28.1 Case Study 1: Overcoming ARFID through Gradual Exposure and Sensory Integration

Background: A 7-year-old boy with autism was diagnosed with Avoidant/Restrictive Food Intake Disorder (ARFID) due to his extreme selectivity in food. He would only eat a handful of bland, texture-free foods, avoiding any foods that were unfamiliar or had complex textures. His parents were concerned about his nutritional intake, and his restricted diet led to significant weight loss.

Intervention: The treatment team, including a pediatrician, nutritionist, occupational therapist, and psychologist, developed a comprehensive plan to address the child's ARFID. The plan included:

- **Gradual Food Introduction**: The team started by introducing small, manageable changes to the boy's diet. They began with foods that had similar textures to his preferred foods and slowly introduced new flavors, with the aim of reducing his anxiety around unfamiliar foods.
- **Sensory Integration Therapy**: Occupational therapy helped address sensory sensitivities to texture, smell, and appearance of food. The child participated in activities that desensitized his tactile and olfactory systems, such as playing with different food textures (e.g., mashed potatoes, jelly) without the pressure of eating them.

- **Positive Reinforcement**: The treatment team used a reward-based system to encourage the boy to try new foods. Small rewards were given when he attempted a new food, and over time, he became more comfortable with the idea of eating a variety of foods.

-

Outcome: After six months, the boy had successfully incorporated a broader range of foods into his diet. He began eating fruits, vegetables, and proteins that he had previously avoided, and his weight stabilized. His family also reported a significant reduction in mealtime stress and an improved relationship with food.

28.2 Case Study 2: Managing PICA with Behavioral Therapy and Environmental Modifications

Background: A 10-year-old girl with autism was diagnosed with PICA, the compulsion to eat non-food items. She frequently ingested inedible objects, such as paper, dirt, and even small plastic toys. This behavior led to multiple health scares, including a hospital visit after ingesting a plastic object that caused a blockage in her digestive tract.

Intervention: The treatment plan involved both behavioral therapy and changes to her environment to reduce opportunities for engaging in PICA:

- **Behavioral Therapy**: The girl's team implemented Applied Behavior Analysis (ABA) techniques to reduce the PICA behavior. They used a combination of positive reinforcement for appropriate behaviors and gentle redirection when she attempted to ingest non-food items. The focus was on reinforcing alternative behaviors, such as using a fidget toy or engaging in a sensory activity, when she felt the urge to eat inedible items.
- **Environmental Modifications**: To reduce triggers, the family modified their home environment by removing non-food items from easy access, increasing supervision during certain activities, and providing her with sensory-friendly, safe alternatives like chew toys or textured materials to satisfy her sensory needs.

- **Parental Training and Support**: The parents received training on how to manage PICA at home and reinforce the behavioral techniques recommended by the therapist. This training helped them maintain consistency in their approach and monitor progress.
-

Outcome: Over the course of a year, the girl significantly reduced her PICA behaviors. She no longer attempted to ingest inedible items, and her family reported fewer medical emergencies. The introduction of safe sensory alternatives also helped her express her sensory needs in healthier ways.

28.3 Case Study 3: Overcoming Food Sensitivities and Expanding Diet in an Adolescent with Autism

Background: A 14-year-old adolescent girl with autism exhibited extreme food selectivity. She had a diet consisting primarily of processed snacks and a limited number of familiar foods. She was resistant to eating anything that didn't fit her strict criteria, and her social life was affected by her unwillingness to eat at family gatherings or school events.
Intervention: The team of professionals focused on expanding her food repertoire while addressing her sensory sensitivities:
- **Cognitive Behavioral Therapy (CBT)**: The adolescent participated in CBT to explore the emotional and cognitive factors driving her food selectivity. The therapist worked with her on recognizing and managing anxiety around food, encouraging gradual steps toward trying new foods.
- **Sensory Integration and Gradual Food Exposure**: The occupational therapist used sensory integration techniques to help the girl tolerate new textures and flavors. She was exposed to new foods through non-threatening methods, like touching, smelling, and observing the food before actually tasting it.
- **Family and Peer Involvement**: The family played a critical role by providing positive reinforcement when the adolescent successfully tried a new food. They also encouraged her participation in group meals, such as potlucks with friends or family dinners, where the focus was on social interaction rather than eating.

Outcome: Over the course of several months, the girl gradually began to incorporate new foods into her diet, including vegetables, fruits, and lean proteins. Her social interactions improved, as she felt more confident eating in public settings. The focus on reducing anxiety around food led to increased flexibility in her eating habits.

28.4 Case Study 4: Successful Collaboration and Long-Term Management of Eating Disorders in ASD

Background: A 9-year-old boy with autism had struggled with both ARFID and PICA for several years, leading to significant nutritional deficiencies and frequent hospitalizations due to ingesting harmful non-food items. His parents were overwhelmed and uncertain how to manage his complex needs. **Intervention**: The family sought help from an integrated team of specialists who used a holistic approach to address both the eating disorder and the autism-related challenges:

- **Comprehensive Assessment**: The team conducted a thorough assessment that included medical tests, nutritional evaluations, and an in-depth review of the child's behavioral patterns. This allowed them to develop a personalized treatment plan.
- **Behavioral and Cognitive Therapies**: A combination of ABA and CBT was used to manage the child's eating disorders. ABA focused on reinforcing healthy eating behaviors and reducing PICA, while CBT helped address the child's food-related anxieties.
- **Nutritional Support**: The nutritionist worked with the family to ensure the child's dietary needs were met, including providing supplements and alternative sources of nutrition when the child was unwilling to consume certain foods. The team also helped the family set up meal plans that were both balanced and acceptable to the child.

Outcome: After a year of combined therapies, the boy showed
marked improvement in both his ARFID and PICA behaviors.
His diet expanded to include a variety of fruits, vegetables, and
proteins, and the frequency of PICA behaviors decreased
significantly. The family reported a much higher quality of life,
with fewer hospital visits and greater peace around mealtimes.
The success was attributed to the ongoing support and
collaboration between the family, healthcare providers, and
therapists.

28.5 Conclusion: The Power of Hope and Perseverance

These success stories demonstrate that with the right treatment
plan, intervention, and support, individuals with autism can
successfully manage eating disorders such as ARFID and
PICA. While progress can take time, the key to success lies in
individualized approaches, involving a team of professionals,
and ensuring consistent support from family and caregivers. By
sharing these success stories, we hope to inspire other families
and individuals on the autism spectrum to continue their journey
toward improved eating habits and overall health, reinforcing the
belief that challenges can be overcome with dedication,
understanding, and a supportive community.

Chapter 29

Long-Term Management and Resilience

Successfully managing eating disorders like ARFID and PICA in individuals with autism requires long-term commitment, flexibility, and resilience from both the individual and their support network. While progress can be made, setbacks are common, and it's crucial to maintain a balanced approach to ensure sustained success. This chapter will explore strategies for long-term management, how to cope with challenges, and ways to build resilience in individuals with autism to navigate their eating behaviors and thrive over time.

29.1 The Importance of Consistency and Flexibility

Managing eating disorders on the autism spectrum is a long-term process that involves balancing consistency with the ability to adapt to new circumstances:

- **Consistency**: Establishing consistent routines around mealtimes, food introductions, and therapeutic strategies is vital for success. This includes keeping a predictable environment where the individual can feel safe and know what to expect. Regular mealtimes, structured food exposures, and consistent reinforcement of desired behaviors help reinforce positive changes over time.
- **Flexibility**: While consistency is important, it's also necessary to remain flexible. Life circumstances may change, and the individual's needs may evolve. Being open to adjusting treatment plans or approaches allows for continuous progress. For example, if a particular food exposure strategy becomes less effective, trying a different approach may yield better results.

29.2 Identifying and Managing Setbacks

It's natural for setbacks to occur along the journey of managing eating disorders, especially in cases involving autism. Learning how to manage these setbacks is key to long-term success:

- **Expecting Setbacks**: Setbacks are part of the process, whether it's a temporary increase in restrictive eating or a return to PICA behaviors. Recognizing that setbacks do not signify failure helps to maintain motivation and reduce stress.

- **Emotional Support**: Both the individual with autism and their caregivers may experience frustration or discouragement when setbacks occur. It's important to offer emotional support and reassurance. Practicing self-compassion and maintaining realistic expectations can help navigate the emotional challenges that come with setbacks.
- **Reevaluating the Approach**: If a setback occurs, it's an opportunity to reassess the situation. Were there any changes in the individual's routine or environment that might have contributed to the setback? Are there new triggers that need to be addressed? Reevaluating the treatment plan and making necessary adjustments is crucial for continued progress.

29.3 Building Resilience in the Individual

Resilience refers to the ability to cope with challenges and bounce back after setbacks. Building resilience in individuals with autism can significantly enhance their ability to manage eating disorders over the long term:

- **Encouraging Self-Awareness**: Helping individuals develop an awareness of their food-related behaviors and emotions can empower them to make decisions that support their well-being. For example, they might learn to identify when they feel anxious about food or when they experience the urge to engage in PICA, allowing them to communicate these feelings rather than resorting to harmful behaviors.
- **Promoting Coping Strategies**: Teaching coping strategies such as deep breathing, mindfulness, or using sensory toys to self-regulate can reduce stress and anxiety around food. These strategies can help individuals stay grounded in moments of distress, preventing emotional overwhelm and impulsive behaviors.

- **Celebrating Small Wins**: Recognizing and celebrating small successes is vital in building resilience. Whether it's trying a new food, reducing restrictive eating behaviors, or resisting the urge to engage in PICA, acknowledging these achievements fosters a sense of accomplishment. Positive reinforcement can be a powerful tool in encouraging continued progress and building self-esteem.

29.4 Building a Supportive Network

Long-term management of eating disorders in autism is not something that should be faced alone. Building a strong, supportive network is crucial for resilience:

- **Family and Caregiver Support**: Caregivers and family members play an essential role in long-term success. They can offer consistent emotional support, participate in therapy sessions, and help with daily management of eating routines. Building a strong support system is crucial for both the individual and the caregivers to prevent burnout and maintain progress.
- **Professional Support**: Continued support from healthcare professionals—such as nutritionists, occupational therapists, behavioral therapists, and psychologists—can help ensure the individual receives the appropriate care as their needs change over time. Regular follow-ups and adjustments to the treatment plan are key to sustained progress.
- **Peer and Community Support**: Joining support groups for families or individuals facing similar challenges can provide a sense of community and reduce feelings of isolation. Peer support can offer practical advice, emotional encouragement, and shared experiences that help families and individuals stay resilient in the face of challenges.

29.5 Long-Term Health Monitoring and Self-Care

As eating habits improve, maintaining long-term health is a priority:

- **Regular Health Check-ups**: Ongoing medical evaluations, including nutritional assessments and health screenings, are necessary to ensure that the individual's physical health is maintained. Regular check-ups help identify and address any emerging issues before they become more serious.
- **Balanced Nutrition**: Ensuring a balanced diet remains a priority. Nutritionists can help create meal plans that focus on both expanding the individual's food choices and meeting their nutritional needs. Supplements may be needed to address any lingering deficiencies.
- **Mindful Mealtime Practices**: Practicing mindful eating—focusing on the sensory experience of eating and tuning into the body's hunger and fullness cues—can help prevent unhealthy food habits from developing over time. This is especially important in the long-term management of eating disorders on the spectrum.

29.6 Maintaining Progress through Patience and Persistence

Ultimately, managing eating disorders like ARFID and PICA in individuals with autism is an ongoing journey that requires patience and persistence:

- **Consistency in Approach**: Although it may take time to see results, consistent effort is key to making lasting progress. Persistence pays off, even when progress seems slow or uneven.
- **Adapting to Growth and Change**: As the individual grows, their needs and preferences may change. What works at one stage of development may need to be adjusted at another. Remaining open to adapting interventions based on the individual's changing circumstances will ensure long-term success.

- **Celebrating Progress**: Taking time to reflect on the journey and celebrate how far the individual has come—no matter how small the achievement—can motivate continued progress. This celebration of growth fosters a sense of self-worth and encourages resilience in the face of future challenges.

29.7 Conclusion: Empowering Individuals to Thrive

The long-term management of eating disorders in individuals with autism requires a multifaceted approach that combines consistency, flexibility, emotional support, and resilience-building strategies. By building a strong support network, adapting treatment plans, and celebrating progress, individuals with autism and their families can navigate the challenges of eating disorders and build a healthier relationship with food. With perseverance and dedication, the journey towards a balanced and fulfilling life is not only achievable but empowering for both the individual and their caregivers.

Chapter 30

Concluding Thoughts: Embracing Individuality

As we conclude this exploration of eating disorders on the autism spectrum—ranging from ARFID and PICA to other eating challenges—it's essential to recognize the unique nature of each individual's journey. Every person with autism has their own story, struggles, and triumphs, and their relationship with food is deeply personal. This chapter emphasizes the importance of embracing individuality, celebrating progress, and fostering an environment of acceptance and patience.

30.1 Embracing Individuality in Eating Behaviors

One of the central themes throughout this book is the importance of recognizing and honoring the individuality of each person on the autism spectrum. Eating behaviors, like all aspects of autism, can vary greatly from person to person. There is no one-size-fits-all approach to managing eating challenges. Some individuals may struggle with sensory sensitivities, while others might display rigid food preferences or even the desire to eat non-food items.
It's crucial to accept that these challenges are part of who the person is. Rather than viewing eating behaviors through the lens of what's "normal" or "acceptable," it's helpful to focus on what's meaningful for the individual. By recognizing and respecting their unique sensory experiences, preferences, and triggers, we can better support their needs and work with them to find strategies that feel right for them.

30.2 The Power of Patience

Managing eating challenges, whether it's ARFID, PICA, or other restrictive eating habits, takes time. For individuals with autism, even small changes can take months—or even years—to fully develop. This journey is not linear, and progress is often slow and incremental. Therefore, patience is not just a virtue—it's a necessity.

Patience is needed from caregivers, healthcare providers, and the individual themselves. There will be times of frustration when progress seems minimal or when setbacks occur. However, it's during these moments that patience can create the space for growth. Every small step forward is meaningful, and it's important to stay committed to the process, even if it feels like it's moving at a slow pace.

30.3 Celebrating Progress, No Matter How Small

A core aspect of promoting success in managing eating disorders on the autism spectrum is celebrating every achievement, no matter how small it may seem. Whether it's trying a new food, reducing restrictive eating behaviors, or even a small improvement in mealtime behavior, these accomplishments should be acknowledged and celebrated. Celebrating progress boosts confidence and self-esteem. For individuals with autism, seeing that their efforts are recognized and appreciated helps reinforce positive behaviors and strengthens their commitment to overcoming eating challenges. It also encourages a positive attitude towards food, mealtimes, and personal growth. Celebrating progress helps create a culture of success and motivation rather than focusing on the difficulties or failures.

30.4 Building a Supportive Environment

Creating an environment that nurtures individuality and celebrates progress requires a supportive network. This includes family members, caregivers, teachers, therapists, and healthcare professionals, all of whom must work together to ensure the individual's needs are met.
Supportive environments are built on the foundations of trust, patience, and understanding. These environments encourage individuals to feel safe and supported as they explore new foods, routines, and behaviors. By fostering a calm, predictable, and accepting atmosphere, we provide the emotional security necessary for individuals with autism to engage in new experiences, including expanding their eating habits.

30.5 The Role of Self-Acceptance

Self-acceptance is a critical element in managing eating challenges and improving overall well-being. When individuals with autism accept themselves and their unique eating behaviors, they can begin to feel more empowered in their journey. Instead of feeling pressured to conform to societal expectations of eating or behavior, they can focus on their own health and comfort.

For caregivers, supporting self-acceptance means encouraging an individual's agency in their food choices and respecting their autonomy. This fosters self-confidence and a sense of control, which is especially important for individuals who may already struggle with anxiety or low self-esteem.

30.6 Redefining Success

Success in managing eating disorders on the spectrum doesn't look the same for everyone. For some, it may be the gradual introduction of new foods. For others, it might mean achieving a level of comfort with food without the compulsion to engage in PICA. Success is not about achieving a "perfect" eating pattern, but rather about progress, learning, and growth at an individual pace.

Redefining success involves setting realistic, achievable goals tailored to the person's abilities and preferences. It's about creating a path where every achievement—no matter how small—is seen as a success and every challenge is an opportunity for learning.

30.7 Moving Forward with Hope

The journey to manage eating disorders like ARFID and PICA in individuals with autism can be challenging, but it's also filled with hope. With the right strategies, tools, and support, individuals can make significant strides in developing healthier relationships with food. Along the way, it's important to remember that the process is as much about the journey as it is about the outcome.

As caregivers, professionals, and individuals with autism continue to work together, there is always room for progress. The future is full of possibilities for those who embrace their individuality, are patient with themselves, and celebrate the small victories along the way.

With love, dedication, and understanding, we can create an environment where individuals with autism feel empowered to make their own choices, enjoy diverse foods, and ultimately thrive. Their journey is theirs to define, and every step forward is a testament to their resilience and strength.

30.8 Conclusion: A Future of Acceptance and Growth

In the end, managing eating challenges on the autism spectrum is about more than just food—it's about fostering a life filled with understanding, acceptance, and growth. It's about supporting individuals in their unique paths, celebrating every victory, and helping them navigate the obstacles that may arise along the way. Together, we can build a future where individuals with autism feel empowered to embrace their individuality, pursue their goals, and experience a fuller, more fulfilling life.

Embrace the journey, trust in the process, and always celebrate progress, no matter how small.

 www.ingramcontent.com/pod-product-compliance
Lightning Source LLC
Chambersburg PA
CBHW051606250726
48653CB00004BA/1372